Sarc

MADE

FOR

HOPE

*Discovering Unexpected Gifts
in Brokenness*

PRAISE FOR *MADE FOR HOPE*

Sara's bravery and honesty in telling her story make *Made for Hope* a compelling and impactful read. As a personal friend of Sara's, who already knew most of these stories before reading the book, I still couldn't put it down! It was that well-written and moving! Sara's expression of her own heartbreak, joy, growth, and faith challenged and encouraged me in my own life and faith. Sara lives what she writes, and that may be the most wonderful aspect of her story. She has truly modeled what it looks like to be made for hope. I can't wait to see the impact and influence her words will undoubtedly leave on many hearts.

—**Christy Cabe**, author, *Brownie Crumbs and Other Life Morsels* and *If Only It Were a Piece of Cake*

So many times, stories about loss leave us despondent and fearful. Sara and Sam's journey with their son, Silas, is a reflection of grace and soulful resilience. What a joy to hear their testimony as a song of victory and not merely a test of survival. As readers, you will be blessed by the beautiful authenticity of emotion, expressed through a young couple's pursuit of God's calling to live in family.

—**Dr. Sherilyn Emberton**, President, Huntington University

Made for Hope tells an achingly beautiful story full of twists, turns, and tragedies and one woman's fierce determination to discover God in every unexpected place. This is the story of faith we all need when we find ourselves carrying the unbearable weight of grief and tiring from our attempts to navigate a new life course that we feel so utterly unprepared for. Through her vulnerable storytelling and as one who understands pain and brokenness, Sara Ward comes alongside the reader as a guide who points us to the one true guide we have in Jesus and encourages us to see that we are made for hope.

—**Kristin Vanderlip**, author, *Life Worth Living: A Daily Growth Journal*

This book is a gift to anyone who reads it. I cried alongside Sara in her pain and rejoiced in her blessings and victories! Her words were so beautifully crafted that I didn't want to put the book down. Not only is this story a work of art, it pulls at every emotion you have. *Made For Hope* is the perfect example of how God uses all things for good.

—**Vanessa Luu**, author, *You Don't Have To Be Perfect*

Sara Ward's comforting and gentle style carries you through the heart-break of a profound loss, but just as gently she lifts your gaze toward hope found in new chapters of her life, and even more importantly, in Jesus and his promises of a joyous tomorrow. This beautifully written book will be an incredible encouragement to many who read it and share in Sara's story.

—**Jeff Jacobson**, author, *I Have (Had) Enough: Memoirs of Abundance in Fatherhood, Friendship, and Faith* and *So I Go Now: Following After the Jesus of Our Day*

In sharing her "before and after" stories, Sara weaves a tapestry of how relationships, nature, and God's Word fit together. Therein are found the essential ingredients of life in a broken world. As a result, we discover hope. Sara's vulnerability and gift of providing vivid word pictures draw the reader into deep emotions and thoughts. Whether you are going through tough times or wanting to come alongside someone who is, this book is eye-opening. It provides a perspective that addresses the reality of suffering, rather than pretending all is fine. Sara says, "All of us need to find those people who are willing to enter our pain." Reading her story will help you be that person or discover how to find that person. I benefitted so much from this book and am certain you will as well.

—**Twyla Lee**, LCSW, social work educator, Intentional Relationships co-consultant and speaker

Through this modern-day Job story, Sara helps us to realize that even
in life's darkest valleys we were made for hope!

—**Julie Rupp**, podcast host, *Parenting Tomorrow's Leaders*

Made for Hope is a story that weaves us through life's most bitter and
joyous events. Sewn together with grace and a bounty of determination to see through her pain, Sara allows us into her deepest fears and
heartbreak so that we can come out on the other side with hope. It is
here we find assurance that indeed God is with us even in our darkest
moments. Sara's extraordinary gift for storytelling allows us to face our
own fears and realize that we, too, are made for hope.

—**Lori Clounie**, blogger, *Only God*, loriclounie.com

Authenticity. Sara tells her story with vulnerable authenticity. She
brings you with her as she journeys through loss, heartbreak, grief, joy
and hope. A great validation for all those who have grieved the death
of a loved one or a dream unrealized and a wonderful tribute to her
son, Silas. Prepare to be blessed.

—**Jane Munk**, MA, MBA, founder of Kerith Brook Retreats for
Grieving Adults

Made for Hope: Discovering Unexpected Gifts in Brokenness

Published in 2019 by Poets and Saints Publishing

ISBN 978-1-7334110-0-4 (print)
ISBN 978-1-7334110-1-1 (ebook)

Cover design and interior design by Kristen Ingebretson
Author photograph copyright © 2019 by Reagan25 Photography.
Edited by Jaci Miller

Some names and identifying details have been changed to protect the identities of persons in the book. While the author has aimed to provide accurate information, some details like websites and other details may have changed. The author assumes no responsibility for author or third-party websites or their content.

For Sam

*You have spoken truth to my heart and
have shown me Jesus' love so well.*

CONTENTS

"Everything can change in an instant.
Everything.
And then there is only
before and after."

Phyllis Reynolds Naylor

INTRODUCTION

began writing this book as a journey through my own loss. In the process, I found a community of people who suffered other kinds of losses: the loss of a spouse, an unborn child, parents, a marriage. All different. All devastating. Every type of loss involves grief, and in a sense, a separation from life as we once knew it.

My son died on October 5, 2012, from a terminal genetic disease. He was almost three years old. For months, I poured out my emotions into words. As I worked through my grief, I was able to process the complexities of pain, suffering, and healing through the lens of writing. I couldn't understand how I was feeling except when I wrote things down. The process forced me to observe my grief in the midst of moments that were still beautiful: the red leaves like a fountain of bleeding color on the horizon, the soft shoot of green bursting through the black frozen dirt of winter. Just as a crucible refines silver under intense heat, my soul had been refined through hardship and pain. Though I would always bear the scars of grief, I began to see hidden treasures from this trial, the gifts that come from brokenness.

This book is a journey chronicling those gifts along the way, in the hope of not just focusing on the valley, but finding out what can be learned there.

Maybe you're wanting to understand why something tragic happened in your life. Perhaps you're trying to see if anything good could come from your disappointments. Death, disease, and brokenness are all part of our fallen world and we may never understand why we went through a particular difficulty.

Instead, how we face our hard times can be transformative. When we turn to Jesus, only then will we find gifts that develop from our deep love of Christ. Through that process, God can redeem the brokenness of a shattered heart and write our stories with a redemptive ending.

I've met people who have not only embraced their pain, but were willing to be fully transformed by it. Their tragedy, and the process of healing, became the catalyst for incredible growth and a deeper relationship with Christ.

The question is not whether we will face hard times, but how we will respond to them. By seeking Jesus in the wreckage of our lives, we can experience Christ as our source of hope, so we can say like the Psalmist, "But as for me, I will always have hope" (Psalm 71:14a).

This is a chance to take your heartache and find redemption in it. This is an opportunity to find unexpected gifts in brokenness and to discover how you were made for hope after all.

PART ONE

Before

I am waiting for the day
when all the sad things
come untrue
when all the mourning
turns to dancing
when all the tears
are only for joy
when I can finally
cup your face in my hands
and never say goodbye again.

ONE

No Going Back

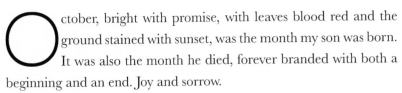

October, bright with promise, with leaves blood red and the ground stained with sunset, was the month my son was born. It was also the month he died, forever branded with both a beginning and an end. Joy and sorrow.

I was in the shower when I heard Sam calling my name. I wanted to ignore the voice, let the water take me away to where yesterday didn't exist. But the voice kept calling, interrupting my thoughts, forcing me to process everything that had happened the day before yesterday. That horrible day.

The door to the bathroom opened. "Where is your purse?" my husband asked.

"It's in the closet downstairs," I replied.

"Are you sure that's where you left it? Because I already checked and it's not there."

"I think it's there," I replied. "That's where I put it every night."

"I came downstairs this morning and the back door to the garage was open, and so was the door from the garage to the patio." Sam's voice sounded urgent. "My phone is missing. So is your purse. I think someone broke in last night."

"What?" I turned off the water and wrapped myself in a towel as water dripped from my hair all over the floor. This had to be a mistake.

I put on my bathrobe and hurried down the steps. When I opened the closet door, the hook that held my purse was empty. I walked to the back door and stared. The door hung wide open, like someone had rushed out of the house and forgotten to close it.

It wasn't hard to figure out how they had entered our home. The outside door to the garage had been locked and was forced open, but the door from the garage to the kitchen had been unlocked. We had been making funeral plans and failed to lock the back door when we went to bed. Someone had taken advantage of our distraction, forced their way into our garage, and then entered our home. The timing couldn't have been worse.

"They took your iPad and iPhone," Sam said. "All the drawers to the buffet were hanging open too."

I shivered as I stood in the door, the cold air pouring into the house.

"I think we need to look around and see what's missing and I'll call the police," he said.

I wasn't ready to face the police again after calling them two days before. I wanted to crawl back into the shower and let the water wash this nightmare away.

I knew that having my purse stolen wasn't the worst thing that could happen to a person. If this break-in hadn't been so close to our other tragedy, I might have thought being a victim of a crime was the worst thing. But I had learned there is a hierarchy of bad-to-worsts, and just when you think things are bad, they can always get worse. I had no idea, two days before, that we were about to hit rock bottom. We lived so unaware of the goodness of life until something came along and shattered everything.

Only two days before, my two-year-old son, Silas, was cocooned in his bed, sleeping off an ear infection. He had a disease called Leigh's, a genetic condition he would not survive. Although his disease always worsened when he was ill, after four doctor's visits and some strong antibiotics, we thought he'd pull through. We went to bed Thursday night hopeful that a good night's sleep would bring some improvement and help us avoid a trip to the emergency room. The ER was always a crapshoot for kids who had complicated and mysterious diseases. Most doctors looked at me blankly when I told them his medical history. Nurses had to ask me how to spell Leigh's because they had never seen it before. This was not a question of their medical qualifications—it just proved that the disease was so rare, most doctors had never encountered it before. Their expertise in treating Silas equated to throwing darts in the dark.

I knew something was not right when I woke up Friday morning and checked on him. By the time we got to the hospital, Silas had stopped breathing altogether. Our son was gone, but I could not leave his side.

Now, only forty-eight hours later, I stared at the open door, the first of several signs that our home had been burglarized. I walked to the closet and saw the empty hook where my purse had hung. I walked into the kitchen where an iPad and iPhone sat charging the night before. All that was left were their charging cords. The drawers of the buffet were pulled out, hanging open like someone had hastily searched for something.

Sam's shoulders slumped. "I'll call the police."

"I can't believe this is happening," I said. I tried to wrap my head around this intrusion. Someone had broken into our home on Saturday night while we slept—or rather, while we tossed and turned in our grief-stricken state—and taken our electronics and my purse. How was it even possible? At some point in the night I had heard a noise, but I decided it was the puppy, who was kenneled for the night, and I hadn't even bothered getting up.

I realized, with a shudder, if I had checked on the sound or woken my husband, we might have put ourselves in a direct confrontation with the intruder. As bad as it was to be robbed, what might have happened could have been so much worse.

Sam called the police while I sat on the edge of the bed, a heaviness weighing on my chest. We were not only dealing with the loss of a child, but our home and security had been violated.

When a police car pulled up, Sam opened the door and discovered it was the same policewoman who had been at our house only forty-eight hours earlier.

"I'm so sorry," she said.

She filled out a police report and took some fingerprints, noting how the thief had moved through our home, first rifling through our car in the garage and then entering our home through the unlocked door. We had made the thief's job easy. Our grief had become his lucky break.

When we had crawled into our bed last night, our eyes puffy from crying and our bodies weak with exhaustion, we hadn't been thinking of what we needed to do before going to sleep. We only thought of our son and how much we missed him.

The policewoman searched the property and found a baby monitor camera thrown behind our storage shed. It was an extra one so I could see Silas in his wheelchair in the kitchen. The camera was located on top of our cabinets with only a tiny green light glowing from it. The thief apparently had thought the camera was a security cam, cut the wires, and disposed of it outside.

"Why did this happen?" I asked.

"You were targeted because of the ambulance call," she replied, like it was a neat and tidy mystery to be solved. The policewoman left with fingerprints but doubted anything would come of it. Unless one of our devices turned up at a pawnshop, they likely would not find the criminal. Truthfully, we didn't care about the stuff we had lost. We wanted our son back.

Soon afterward, my neighbor knocked on our front door. He'd discovered my purse behind their back fence, its contents strewn all over the ground. The thief hadn't taken any of my credit cards and only managed to pocket the three dollars I had in my wallet. We thanked our neighbor, but I did not want the purse back. It was now contaminated by someone who had invaded my home and rifled through my things. I hung it in the closet, unsure what to do with it.

I sat on my bed, wondering what had happened to my life in two short days. I had lost my son, my house had been robbed, and now I was left with a purse that had been ripped apart and thrown in the weeds, which was how I felt too, like someone had ripped my heart open and thrown it in the weeds.

It was, at that moment, that I realized what rock bottom felt like. Contrary to what people believed, I hadn't realized I had hit rock bottom in the hospital when my son died. At that point, I was in too much shock, just trying to breathe. Only later did I find rock bottom in an ordinary moment that reminded me of what life used to be, before everything went wrong, before life as I knew it disappeared.

A few days later, another neighbor stopped by, holding a soft, camel tan leather purse. She told me that a woman from work heard my story and felt compelled to give me a handbag she never used.

"She knew you might feel uncomfortable about using the one that had been stolen," my neighbor said. "She thought you might like to use something different." She handed me the impeccable bag that looked like it fell straight out of a designer magazine.

"Thank you," I said, floored that a stranger would want to give me a purse, but even more, that she would understand how I felt about using a stolen one. It was my first lesson about the kindness of strangers in the midst of tragedy.

Only a week before, I was pushing my son in his wheelchair to the doctor's office, and like every other time before, I carried my purse with me. The purse hung limply on my shoulder at every doctor's appointment, every hospital stay, every blood draw. Even though it wasn't expensive, it contained what I needed to survive—my money, my identity, a cell phone.

But now everything was wrong. Someone had shaken loose my whole life, just like the purse behind the fence, spilling everything into a chaotic mess. Before today, the bag had no sentimental value, but now it represented the life I had before my son died, when I didn't know what I had.

The truth was, we can't ever know ahead of time when our lives will be divided in half, when there will only be before and after. Our worlds can be split into two, like a piece of wood beneath the wedge of an axe. My life had started a new chapter, and looking at the purse, I realized the loss of everything that came before.

I had no idea how I would go on or how I would pick up the pieces of my own life. I only knew what I had to do next. I picked up the stolen purse and walked out the back door of the house into the crisp fall air. After crossing the patio, I opened the lid to the trash can and tossed the purse inside.

The life I had before was gone, and there was no going back now.

TWO

When Your Life Is Split in Two

———————————————

grew up in a small town in Indiana where the corn grew high and cars dodged Amish buggies on the potholed country roads. I played in the church cemetery after the worship service on sunny days while the adults chatted in the foyer. Sometimes we gathered in the church basement after service, our moms hauling in avocado-green Crockpots and foil-covered casserole dishes, so that we feasted on a potluck lunch of various mushroom soup casseroles and gelatin salads featuring suspended mandarin oranges or shaved carrots.

Donning white gloves and a hat on Easter Sunday, I sat in a Sunday school room with four or five other kids, while Mabel, a single woman with greying hair, taught us Bible stories. Even in that familiar space I was still too scared to recite my Bible verse out loud, so I would whisper it in Mabel's ear, like a prayer.

We rode bikes down country roads, without helmets, because no one I knew wore a helmet or buckled their seatbelt in the back of the car. We made our own homemade dirt bike path in the woods, before excavators came through and took out the trees for a housing development.

In those days, there wasn't much to do in the summer unless you wanted to play softball at the local ball diamond. We ate bologna sandwiches on fluffy white bread with square cheese slices, and when we ran out of bologna, there was always Spam in the cupboard. There were no day camps, no enrichment classes, no sports clubs, no summer arts programs. We were free as birds and roamed the fields and woods like a pack of wild dogs. Most kids stayed home on hot summer afternoons, jumping sprinklers in the backyard or playing with neighbor kids. If you were lucky, you got to swim at the neighbor's pool, where you spent the afternoon burning to a gentle pink hue that eventually turned a light shade of brown, complete with swimsuit strap tan lines.

When I was five, we moved into a new ranch home, in what was to become a subdivision in a cornfield. Modern suburbia was penetrating our rural town, but as a child, I saw the expanding neighborhood as an opportunity to make new friends to play with during long Sunday afternoons when my dad snored in his brown leather recliner, the newspaper rising and falling on his chest.

I hoped this new friend also came with a swimming pool, since my two greatest dreams in life were owning a pool and a horse. Since my parents had no intentions of buying either one, I was given *The Black Stallion* for my birthday and a Barbie pool instead. It was the era of Ronald Reagan and boom boxes, permed hair and Walkman tape players.

My father worked as a quality control manager at a dairy during the day and volunteered on the ambulance crew at night. He looked at bacteria under microscopes and brought home Petri dishes growing with strange substances, which he placed in our refrigerator. His job was to make sure dairy products were safe for human consumption, so when he arrived home with the Petri dishes, he gave strict instructions not to eat what was growing inside.

In the evening, he carried a small radio around when he was on call for the volunteer ambulance crew. It came on with a loud piercing wail, interrupting our dinner. When I heard the signal, I became aware that someone, somewhere was in need of help. My dad raced out to his car, plugged in a blue emergency light into his cigarette lighter, set the light on top of his car, and then drove off into the night, like an episode of *CHiPs*. When he returned, he told tales of rescuing old ladies who had fallen down or elderly men who struggled to breathe. But occasionally, worse things happened, events he kept from me because I was too young to understand.

These tragedies seemed like a separate world, far removed from our home in the suburban development nestled between cornfields and maple trees. These happened to other people and I had no fear about it happening to me. Because my world was still untouched by tragedy, I only saw brokenness like a child looking through a window. At that time, my worst problem was being teased about the home perm my mother had given me. When I stepped on the bus the next morning, twin girls who lived on my street pointed at my hair and howled with laughter. In one agonizing bus ride to school, I realized I no longer wanted my hair permed. I sunk down into my seat and looked out the window, trying to disappear from the taunts. When you are young, the worst things in your life aren't all that bad, but you can only see that in hindsight. In the moment, they feel like catastrophes. Although I was keenly aware of the teasing, my world orbited around tragedy, but never really touched it.

In the same way, my dad witnessed the tragedies on his ambulance calls—the bad car accidents, the heart-attack victims, the elderly who passed away in their sleep—but he only passively participated in the tragedy, an onlooker who helped victims reach the hospital. It was not his tragedy and he did not have to live with the aftermath of it. This was a blessing we did not even know we had.

Then one day, when I was sixteen, my father collapsed suddenly, without any warning, while cleaning out the garage. My mother was making supper, while I played a flute solo from Mendelssohn's *A Midsummer Night's Dream*. We found him, unresponsive, in our driveway. His glasses were knocked off his face. I felt his chest for breathing.

"Run and get the neighbor," Mom said as we stood around him helplessly. My father had been the only one in the family who knew how to perform CPR.

Our wait for the ambulance stretched on as our neighbor tried desperately to revive my father. Finally, sirens blared as the ambulance stopped in front of our house and the crew loaded him in the back. The volunteer ambulance on which my father had served now carried him away.

When we arrived at the hospital, they ushered us into a small, dark wood paneled room at the hospital, separating us from the glaring lights of the ER. Then a doctor walked in, told us he had passed away, and announced the time of death.

"How did he die?" my mother asked, confused by how a normal day could take such a drastic turn.

"An apparent heart attack," the doctor said. "Do you want to see him?"

"Yes," we said and were led to the room where he lay on a table, his face tinged a bluish color. There had not been time for goodbye and what shocked us most, was how we were so unprepared for it all. For our own emergency. For death to touch our family. For the closing of a chapter that we didn't want to end.

By the end of the day, my father was gone, and my life was split in two—a before and after. That is how our time on earth is marked, by births and deaths, by first and last breaths, by beginnings and endings.

On that day I realized that people died, every day, unexpectedly. Although I knew this happened to others, I never thought it would happen to me. Call it a coming-of-age realization, but an awareness of my own mortality dawned on me, a revelation that we are not guaranteed any number of days, no matter how much we think we deserve it.

Later, I heard a story about a man in the Middle East who was in an accident that left him permanently disabled. After many years, the man decided to try to find answers to the question of suffering. Everyone he spoke with believed the accident was meant to happen for a reason. They used an Arabic term called *maktoob* which means, "It was written."[1] The man rejected this idea of maktoob and instead blamed the accident on unfortunate circumstances.

But the man's conclusions left me unsatisfied. If all of life's experiences resulted from carelessness, then what was the purpose behind our pain? In this context, the reasons for our suffering became nonexistent. I found myself there on a cold day in November after the death of my father, fully broken, waiting for answers to my questions, for the acceptance of my own maktoob and the redemption of my pain. Though I did not have understanding yet, I had my faith, my belief that from dust, life would rise.

I believed our lives were written too, documented in Psalm 139 when David wrote,

> Your eyes saw my unformed body;
>
> all the days ordained for me were written in your book
>
> before one of them came to be. (Psalm 139:16)

What I did not know yet, was that this was only the beginning of many more disappointments, where I would search for understanding, for my own maktoob in the middle of a hopeless situation. I wanted to discover, even in brokenness, that there was redemption.

As I stood over my father's body in the hospital, I knew this closed a chapter I did not want to end. I knew this was where I would have to find my way in the world on my own.

THREE

Laying Down Your Dreams

art of finding my way in the world, it turned out, was falling in love. I was still trying to understand the idea that if our bad circumstances were part of maktoob—*it was written*—then so were our good ones.

I met my husband, Sam, during my sophomore year in college. Our paths first crossed when we were acting in a college musical called *Joseph and the Amazing Technicolor Dreamcoat,* a show with such a huge cast, we never talked once through the whole show.

But less than a year later, we were both cast in a small traveling theater show, where I finally got to know this guy who was everything I was not—extroverted, the life of the party, a good debater. It turned out he was interested in getting to know me too, the introverted girl who'd rather stay in than go out, who liked deep conversation over small talk.

When we were back in college after summer break, my roommates started asking why I wasn't dating Sam and I wondered the same thing. A few weeks later, we found ourselves eating Mexican food together on a warm fall evening, the first of many dates. Our love story grew slowly, like a garden planted in deep soil.

A few years later, we married on a cold December day, two days after Christmas. Like most young couples, we mapped out our lives like a jigsaw puzzle, every plan snapping into place with a satisfying click. Although I knew women who struggled with the decision of when they wanted to become a mom, we were on the five-year plan. It all seemed so perfect, I had no idea that planning was not only unnecessary, it wouldn't even matter in the end. It turned out, that this too, was part of what was written.

Growing up, I babysat for two of my nieces, who were completely enamored with Barbie dolls. When they came over, I pulled out a large box stuffed full of Barbies and their accessories, from elaborate party dresses, to dozens of stiletto shoes and fancy hats. But I had learned one important rule for managing expectations: everyone wanted the same dolls, and inevitably, there would be fighting over who got the coveted Barbies.

The easiest way to handle the issue was to have a plan to fairly distribute the dolls, so we numbered the dolls and then drew numbers out of a hat. Since I had an entire box of Barbies, everyone got at least enough Barbies to make a family for the day, and maybe even a few extras to play the support roles, like maid, hairdresser, and best friend. The drawing ensured that you had as much of a chance of gaining the more desirable Barbies as the less desirable ones. If you were particularly unlucky, and drew all the old Barbies with tangled hair and body parts that fell off spontaneously, you made the best of an unfortunate situation. You dressed them in fabulous clothes to draw attention away from the bad hair. You held on to hope that next time you'd get a better draw. Next time, you might even get the lone Ken doll.

Unfortunately, this is not the way life works. We don't get second or third chances to draw a better life when things turn disastrous. Our dreamboat Ken may never show up. Our plan for three adorable babies in the backseat of our silver Corvette might not ever materialize. While my nieces planned dream lives with their Barbies, reality sometimes ends differently. In the end, maktoob still applies to all things big and small, joyous and painful.

Looking back, motherhood was always my goal, but I never remember having a conversation about the reality that some couples struggled with infertility. Maybe I just didn't notice those couples, but it never occurred that this problem could happen to me. I ignored that the world, or my own body, could actually turn on me.

When we tried to start our family and the door slammed in our faces month after month, I struggled with accepting this new path of disappointment. I knew I should be content with my life—that this wasn't just a smart life principle, but a biblical one—yet I felt like I was terrible at actually living it out. How could I ever be content with accepting that I could not have children?

I wanted so badly to feel happy for all my friends' pregnancy announcements, while I grappled with another month of bad news. I wanted to celebrate with them, instead of cringing at another baby shower invitation. It pained me to sit through another bubble-gum pink party while fearing I would be asked, "Are you going to be next?"

I didn't want to talk about our struggles, and yet, I couldn't escape the questions.

"When are you guys planning on having children?" people asked, as if my family planning was any of their business.

I once listened to a group of women discuss in detail how many years apart they wanted to space their children. "When you have three children, you always have an odd number for sitting in restaurants and cars," one woman said.

She was weighing the pros and cons of two versus three children and which one they wanted to choose. They were planning their offspring like they were buying a used car.

I sat there thinking, *I just want one child. Just one.* No matter how hard I tried to forget about it, pray about it, and trust God with it, I constantly dodged emotional bullets. The careless comments. The nosy questions. The unending stream of advice.

When I told close friends we had not been able to get pregnant, they dismissed our problem as "not really that bad." Others would say, "Just relax!" as if reducing stress was the key to conception. Infertility is a medical problem, not a psychological one, but it seemed like nine out of ten people thought otherwise.

One person told us to "go have a glass of wine and relax." It didn't seem to matter that I knew many couples whose lives were very stressful and who, ironically, had no problem getting pregnant.

But I couldn't blame the problem on others. The ultimate problem rested with myself and my view of God. I had a plan and I believed it was a good desire that pleased God, but now God was not fulfilling his end of the deal. Of course, the problem with that view was that life was all about me, when really none of it was about me. I was still learning that God had entirely different plans for our family and that I needed to submit my own desires to him, even though it was a painful transformational process. Giving up a long-awaited dream, especially one that shaped my identity as a woman, formed a deep wound, and one not always recognized by the world around me.

Until I could grieve this loss, I could not get over it and move on. Until I could fully lay down my desire and burn it to ashes and dust, I could not heal from it. Singing "I Surrender All" in church seemed so easy in theory, but in practice, it meant I had to loosen my grip on controlling my life. In other words, I had to let go. I was learning what submission to God's will really was: letting go of what I wanted, so that God could do his work in me.

Each one of us, at some point, will face disappointments. We will not have perfect bodies, perfect spouses, or perfect families. We won't always get what we want. Eventually we make a choice: we learn to find contentment or we live in restless discontent.

I was still finding my way to the first one. That meant realizing that my future was designed by a loving and gracious God who does not leave me alone in my circumstances. He doesn't throw me into the fire and then leave me to flounder there. He is good and won't abandon me to this broken world.

After several tests at the gynecologist's office that came back normal, and at least one attempt at fertility drugs, the doctor finally told me that there wasn't much more he could do. He handed me a card for a fertility clinic. As I took the card, I knew that we were ready to move on, but not to a fertility clinic. Our insurance didn't cover the costs, and on a pastor's salary, we knew we couldn't do both fertility treatments and adoption—it was one or the other.

I already knew where my heart lay. The image of a Haitian girl, sitting outside in the blazing sun, was burned into my mind from years ago, when a tiny seed of adoption was planted in my mind. I had no idea how hard that dream would be to chase or all that I would have to lose in the process, but I was willing to open my heart anyway. Come what may.

FOUR

The Journey to You

———————————————————

We traveled all over the globe in our early years of marriage, staying in an old hostel in London and waking up in a cozy hotel in Paris that served croissants on white plates and espresso in tiny cups. We camped on Cape Cod and hiked up ancient stone steps in Israel. We crossed time zones with two small suitcases and each other. It was all we ever needed. These trips were mostly dreamy and exhilarating, the two of us catching trains in foreign countries and wandering unknown cities with paper maps.

Less than two years into our marriage, before we even thought about starting a family, Sam worked for a college admissions office, where we were asked to chaperone a group of students on a weeklong trip to Haiti.

Although I had never been on a mission trip before, something nudged me to go—never mind that we were barely older than the students we were chaperoning, or that we didn't have a clue about what we would do there. We were young and energetic and too naive to understand that trips like these could be dangerously transformative.

A few months later, we packed our bags and flew to the Caribbean, where we saw the hilly country from the back of a pickup truck, passing Haitians walking with woven baskets and stacks of bananas on their heads. Our job for the week was setting up a mobile Vacation Bible School and teaching children in several small villages.

I had grown up going to VBS as a child, where we created elaborate crafts, a songwriter led music on a guitar, and the church ladies made homemade snacks. Even in our small country church, VBS was a well-planned affair, but the expectations differed here.

We gathered kids for VBS in a way that seemed like something out of the Bremen Town Musicians. The missionaries in Haiti told us to walk the village streets, which were nothing more than dirt paths, and call out to any children we saw. Never mind that we didn't know French Creole and were a bunch of strange foreigners invading their village, or that in America, we would never let a stranger, pacing our street, take our child for a couple hours. Cultural differences were a strange thing and we trusted that the missionary knew what worked.

We started down a dirt path, the hot sun beating down on us, and began calling, "V-B-S" in Creole. At first no one acknowledged us, but we kept walking and calling, and soon, a few curious children came trickling out of their homes, staring at us. Some of the college girls coaxed them over with a wave of their hands and the children followed. It only took a few children tagging behind before more began to follow. Eventually we gathered a group of children walking with us, wanting to know what this VBS stuff was all about.

We were clearly the outsiders, being American, white, and wealthy compared to their standards, despite the fact we were poor college graduates chaperoning equally poor college students. Context is everything, and in this severely impoverished country, we were the privileged ones. But the children we met did not seem deterred by that. They grasped our hands before we knew to offer them and they showed us that even though we felt awkward, they did not. If I hesitated to hold hands at the start of the week, fearing I'd scare them away, I wasn't hesitant by the end of the week.

During one of our workdays, we hopped in the back of a truck bed and traveled to an orphanage to play with the kids. Since we had spent most of our time organizing and running the VBS program, the idea that we just had to show up seemed like an easy diversion. I assumed the orphanage owned toys and games, or at least a ball to organize a game of kickball. But when we arrived the children were sitting in their sleeping quarters: a cement floor with open-air walls and a bedsheet tied up as a privacy curtain. They had no beds or belongings, and to my dismay, no toys.

I wondered how I could possibly entertain a child for an hour with nothing, not even the ability to use words, since I could not speak Creole. As I smiled nervously at the kids, they looked back at us blankly. These weren't the same kids we met in the village who held our hands or ran alongside us to the VBS. These kids had experienced loss upon loss—the loss of their family, on top of the loss of home and any familiar comforts. Their lethargy could have been the result of malnutrition or even exhaustion from the soaring heat, but either way, playing a game of tag was not an option.

At some point, one of us picked up a rough rock that was small enough to fit into the palm of a child's hand, and gave it to one of the children. The child took the rock and hid it in his palm and put his hands behind his back. He then pulled his fists out and presented them to one of the college students. We realized then, he was trying to play a game of guess-which-hand-is-hiding-the-rock and the college student, quick to catch on, tapped one of his hands. The child turned his fist around and opened it, revealing an empty palm. All the kids roared with delight that the adult had been fooled, and the child, who was smiling, hid the rock again. As soon as we saw what was happening, more kids grabbed rocks and we paired up, playing "guess the hand" the rest of the time. As it turned out, we didn't need toys after all, just the rocks under our feet. I had learned my first lesson about children— toys or words are not necessary when earth and sky will suffice.

That same week, I met a tiny, one-year-old girl whose mom worked as a housekeeper at the mission. Because childcare wasn't an option for most Haitian moms, the child sat in a cooking pot in the middle of the yard, while her mom cleaned one of the buildings at the mission. At some point, the mother saw us and tried to tell us that we should take this baby home. At first I couldn't understand what she was saying. *Why would a mother ever suggest this?*

We stammered and said that wasn't possible and let the subject go. There were, after all, laws protecting children against this sort of thing.

Adoption in most countries was highly regulated, designed to protect children and parents and ensure that the whole process proceeded lawfully and ethically. But afterward, I couldn't stop thinking about what she had asked. She saw an opportunity for her daughter to live a different life, where she would not have to sit on a cooking pot in the sweltering heat, or go hungry, or play with rocks. She saw her child with opportunities for education and careers that she would never have. She saw a way out.

No matter how hard I try, I cannot possibly understand what it's like to live in one of the poorest countries on earth. Every day we saw children walking around without any clothes. Women scrubbed their laundry in a river with contaminated water. Families lived in shacks I wouldn't use to house a pet.

One day, I saw a rail thin dog, whose ribs poked out like a skeleton with skin, eating scraps of chicken bones. Everything had been stripped off the bones, but the dog was starving, and because she was also nursing puppies, needed extra nutrition. The dog's teeth cracked against the bones, pulverizing them like candy. In a country where the people were starving, the animals lived on whatever was leftover. Today that dog had bones to eat and that might be enough, but what about tomorrow? I knew the answer, but all I could do was watch the dog demolish the bones. This was what she did to keep her puppies alive.

When our airplane left the Haitian soil, I thought back to the little girl in the pot. I remembered the children in the orphanage who played with rocks. A seed had been planted and an idea rolled in my mind.

At the time, I didn't understand fully what adoption meant or the complications that adoption brings to both biological and adoptive families. I didn't understand that being an adoptive mother was not about saving a child's life. Up until that point, I had never considered what it might be like to form a family this way. But now that I had opened the door, I couldn't seem to close it, like someone had placed a wedge in the door. I had gone on this trip to help children, but instead found that they had changed me.

The seed that was planted on that trip to Haiti was growing into something new. Although some dreams in life fade from existence, others continue to emerge, like a bobber poking up from the surface of a lake.

I was searching for something I didn't quite understand yet, the children I'd call my own, and the path that would lead me to them.

FIVE

When Life Takes a Detour

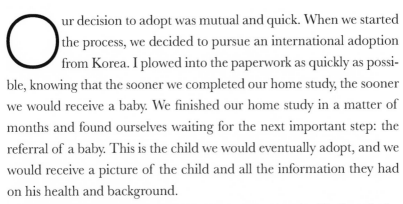

Our decision to adopt was mutual and quick. When we started the process, we decided to pursue an international adoption from Korea. I plowed into the paperwork as quickly as possible, knowing that the sooner we completed our home study, the sooner we would receive a baby. We finished our home study in a matter of months and found ourselves waiting for the next important step: the referral of a baby. This is the child we would eventually adopt, and we would receive a picture of the child and all the information they had on his health and background.

Several months later, Sam started having back pain. He thought he had probably pulled something in his back and needed time to recover. But slowly, over several weeks, the back pain worsened, even though he was trying to rest. His doctor prescribed some pain relievers, but when those didn't touch his pain, his doctor sent him to the ER for tests.

When the ER doctor entered our room to give us the test results, I noticed something: he closed the door. Only afterward did I understand its meaning.

"You have cancer," the doctor said. We sat in uncomfortable silence while the doctor continued with the results. "There is a large mass in your abdomen. We've called an oncologist to look at your CT scan."

"But he is so young, only thirty years old," I told the doctor, as if age made a difference and cancer only afflicted the elderly. How little I knew about the brokenness of life, that we are all only one step away from a terminal diagnosis.

The doctor replied, "I've got a girl in here who's eighteen years old and terminal."

As an emergency room doctor, this was his daily reality. People died every day, whether they were old or young. But this had not been our reality. Our friends were all healthy. They were getting married and having babies. In the prime of life.

"We need to keep your husband overnight," the doctor said and then left the room.

We started making calls, telling our family the news and weeping with them over the phones. Our world had turned upside down with one diagnosis. When we finished, Sam told me to go home and get some sleep. We had nothing with us other than a notebook and my purse. I nodded and told him I'd pack his things and return early in the morning.

When I went home, the doctor's words looped in my mind on an awful, repetitive soundtrack. I thought of the words in my notebook that ended abruptly when the doctor walked in, a reminder of how everything changed in an instant. That is how pain is preceded, by the normal, ordinary rituals of life. I began roaming the house late at night, straightening everything to rid myself of the panicky feeling that my life was spinning out of control. When I finally lay down in bed, I wondered what would happen to Sam. Our adoption. The future. We had been waiting to receive a referral of a baby at any moment, but the diagnosis jeopardized everything. We needed to call the adoption agency to tell them the news, but the thought of it disrupting our plans shattered me. We had waited so long for a child. *Why this? Why now?*

Throughout our marriage, Sam was the rock solid one when I gave into despair. When we faced infertility, he always remained encouraging, reminding me that I would someday be a mother. When we started the adoption journey, he jumped in fully committed with no hesitation. Now I wondered how I could be the strong one in this new normal.

I had been going to church ever since I was born, but only now, as a thirty-year-old, did my faith feel tested in a way I didn't know how to make sense of. I was confronted with the realization that I was either going to lean on God's promises or give in to despair. I was going to doubt God's promises or believe he would carry me through this. If maktoob was true, then this was no surprise for God, even if it was for me. My days were written in his book and there was nothing that was out of his hands.

The next few days were a blur of tests and doctors. We learned the official diagnosis was testicular cancer and that, according to the oncologist, it was one of the few cancers with a high cure rate. Sam would have to endure several months of surgeries and horrendous chemotherapy that would leave him sick, weak, and utterly exhausted.

The doctor recommended we start chemotherapy the same day. There were some difficult decisions to make, namely, whether we wanted to pursue procedures that would make it possible to have biological children down the road. The process would delay chemotherapy for another week, which was risky.

"Talk about it over lunch," the doctor told us. "But if you wait a week, the cancer could spread to your brain."

We ate in a loud, crowded hospital cafeteria, possibly the worst place to discuss a decision about future children. Even though I wanted children, there were some things I would not risk. My husband's life was one of them. We went back to the doctor after lunch and told him we'd start chemotherapy that day.

When we called the adoption agency to tell them the bad news, they told us we could not continue in the Korean adoption program. The country had strict rules about their adoptive parents' health and a recent cancer diagnosis would not be allowed. Even if we had already been matched with a baby, they would have to decline the match. There was nothing they could do.

In a matter of days, our adoption had fallen through and my husband was fighting for his life. One of those surprises alone would have been hard, but both at the same time devastated us. Just a few weeks before, I was imagining us as a family of three, but now I didn't even know if we would remain a family of two.

This was our new reality, one where I had to put on a brave face each day and help Sam get out of bed and put on his clothes. People kept saying how strong I was, but the truth was, I didn't feel strong at all. I just felt broken.

Somehow, in the midst of walking through cancer, I still held on to hope that even though my life might be a mess, God was in control. He still had a plan for our family. We had been told there was a good chance that my husband would beat cancer. When we told our adoption caseworker this news, she replied, "Call us as soon as he is cancer-free."

Her words offered a sliver of hope that our adoption journey was not over.

SIX

One Breath at a Time

———————○

For the next three months, Sam lost his hair, turned ghostly pale, and spent every day sleeping on the couch. I became his full-time caregiver, measuring morphine, helping him out of bed, and buttoning his clothes, because the neuropathy in his fingers had turned viciously painful. The doctor knew that the silver bullet for this particular kind of cancer was an intense, three-month treatment. Hit it hard and fast.

"We'll give you the most chemotherapy a person can take without killing you," the doctor said.

The result devastated both his cancer and his body. His veins hardened to a point where I couldn't touch his arms. But it was the side effects that drained him completely—the horrendous nausea, bone pain, nerve tingling, and exhaustion that made him bone tired. When I brought home fresh strawberries, he gagged so violently on the smell that he told me to get rid of them immediately.

When he wasn't receiving chemotherapy, he slept on the couch, with the cat curled up next to him. The doctor told us that some of the side effects, like exhaustion and nausea, would go away after treatment, but others could be long-term or even permanent. It was a small price to pay for surviving the disease, even though nothing felt small. Everything revolved around survival, getting through another day, counting down how many treatments remained.

Because Sam was too tired to take the stairs, we took the elevator to the third-floor oncologist's office. In a matter of weeks, he had gone from an energetic thirty-year-old, to a balding, old man. On chemotherapy days, he was tethered to an infusion chair for over four hours. I made several trips from the hospital to work and back again, bringing him his lunch and checking on him. During one of those trips, I got on the elevator with strangers, some heading to neurology, others to urology or reproductive medicine. I could usually guess the ones headed to oncology like us. They were often in a wheelchair, bald, or over sixty years old. I was the age of most of their kids.

Once, I found myself in the elevator with a mother and children, who were headed to pediatrics. She juggled a baby on one hip and a toddler stood next to her leg. The baby slept, while the mother watched the floor numbers light up. She had seen her child sleep a million times before, but I marveled at his tiny slumbering body and the serene expression on his face. I realized how similar the bald and exhausted chemo patients looked when sleeping with blankets pulled up to their chins. The toddler on the elevator was trying to push buttons, fiddling with his mother's bags, jumping from leg to leg, until the doors opened and he burst out like a jack-in-the-box. The mother barked orders after him. "Just wait! Don't touch that! Slow down!"

She left and I stayed on the elevator, the door closing between us like a giant wall, the same wall I had tried to climb for years now. I couldn't help but feel that little knot in my stomach, the same tight pull that reminded me most of these women were my age and were headed to pediatrics, while I was headed to oncology.

As the doors closed, I was left alone, on my way to floor three. It made me wonder how I got here, how my life changed in an instant, how I sat with the sick, their veins dripping with heavy metals, toxic to their cancer, poisonous to their own cells, when I should have been getting off at pediatrics.

I used to be afraid of hospitals, of doctors, and everything that went with it—all of it a reminder of my own mortality. Normal life seemed like an out-of-reach blessing now, the humdrum of routine like the beating of a heart. Only now that the rhythm of our lives had been upset did I realize how much I missed it.

As we counted down the months of completing chemotherapy, I watched my friends get pregnant and have babies, buy houses, get new jobs, and go on vacations, while I sat in the oncology unit watching chemo drip into my husband's veins. I listened to his lungs rattling as he slept while I lay awake in the dark. Dying people faced their days the only way they knew how: one breath at a time.

Right before the Fourth of July, we got the call that Sam was finally cancer-free. We were both elated, although he only reacted as a chemo patient could: the news lifted his spirit, but his body still slumped under the exhaustion. We went out for salmon and oysters, and celebrated that we were not at the hospital or a doctor's appointment. We had forgotten how normal people lived.

When we called our adoption agency and told them the good news, they told us that unfortunately Sam's remission would not be good enough for Korea's stringent health standards. The best option for our situation was to switch over to the domestic adoption program in the U.S. We would have to redo some of our paperwork, but at the time, they needed more families in the program because they currently were working with an influx of birth mothers.

We quickly submitted our updated paperwork and created a photo book for birth parents to look at. Within a few months, we got a call that a birth mother was interested in our family. We painted the baby's room a pale green late into the night, hoping that after our tough year, this would finally be our chance to turn things around. We tried to act like life was normal, as if we weren't waiting for a phone call that could change everything.

On a Monday morning a few weeks before the due date, Sam's phone rang. Labor had started and we needed to come as quickly as possible. We ran home, threw our stuff into a bag, and sped down the highway toward the hospital. When we arrived, we found out we had missed the baby's birth. It was a girl. We stopped at the nursery window and watched a nurse bathe our new baby girl.

"Can we see her?" Sam asked one of the nurses.

"You'll have to get one of the security bands downstairs before we can allow it," the nurse replied.

Sam raced downstairs to get our bands while I waited by the window, my face almost touching the glass. In only a few months, our lives had taken yet another U-turn. My chemo-exhausted husband was back to normal. Our shattered adoption plans had been restored. In the midst of the mess, God had never forgotten about us.

When Sam finally returned, we bolted into the nursery, where we took turns holding our new daughter. A nurse had tied a tiny green bow in her curls, the same shade as her newly painted bedroom. Green was the color of spring when the shoots of flowers began piercing the earth. We named her Eliana which meant, "God has answered our prayer."

Several months later, we stopped at a restaurant after Sam's follow-up oncology appointment. Our new daughter was with us, her milky brown skin shining in the light. We sat down in a booth where we met our waitress, Marsha, an African-American woman with wide eyes and a smile to match. When Marsha returned with our drinks, she looked at my daughter and then asked slowly, "Are you babysitting or is she your daughter?"

I paused. Our waitress seemed friendly, but I wasn't sure why she was asking. I looked at Sam. "This is our daughter," he said.

When I looked back at Marsha, she was still smiling, but now she had tears in her eyes. "Can I pray for you?" she asked.

In the middle of the restaurant, our waitress knelt down at our table, held our hands and prayed a blessing over our family. We thanked her before she went back to the kitchen. My husband and I looked at each other and then glanced down at our daughter. Whatever I was expecting from our waitress that day, I wasn't expecting this. The complexity of our journey suddenly seemed to come together, like the pieces of a puzzle snapping into place. Without cancer, we wouldn't be *this* family.

After we finished our lunch, we looked around for Marsha. We didn't want to leave without thanking her, but she had disappeared into the kitchen. Sam walked up to the cashier to pay.

"It's been paid sir," replied the cashier. "Someone was feeling generous today."

Sam looked around and finally spotted Marsha in the back. "Did you pay for our meal?" he asked, grinning.

She just smiled and said, "There are angels all around. All around."

We found out Marsha was right. We kept bumping into these angels at critical times.

A few years later, we began our second adoption journey. After working three jobs to raise adoption funds, we were still short of our goal to pay for the adoption fees. The number was a discouraging amount, but we forged ahead anyway.

The next week at church a guy approached us in the foyer. "My wife and I aren't going to adopt any more children, but we wanted to help families who are adopting, so we would like to send you something."

"Thank you," Sam replied, a little speechless at the man's generosity. We gave him our address and left.

A few days later, Eliana poked along on a slow walk to the mailbox with me, which usually ended with a handful of sale flyers and junk mail. But today, I noticed a white envelope with the name of the guy at church that we met. When we got home, Sam opened the envelope. He looked at the check and handed it to me.

"Oh my word," I said.

The check was for the exact amount of our adoption shortfall. Eliana didn't understand why I was crying in that moment, but she knew God was bringing us a baby. When Sam called the man on the phone to thank him, tears spilled down his face as he told him how much this money meant to us. The last time he cried on the phone was when he called his parents to tell them he had cancer. But this time, his tears were different. In this moment, they were full of joy.

SEVEN

Stay Strong, Mama

W hen life settled down into a constant rhythm of family life, I thought that we had climbed our mountain and made it to the other side. I believed, falsely of course, that we were safe from any sort of big trial, because we had paid our dues and gotten our "get out of suffering" card.

At that time, I thought that life was like the game of Monopoly. With careful planning and a little luck, you could get what you wanted if you made the right choices. Once in a while, you could even receive the "get out of jail free" card, which kept you from landing in jail and gave you a pass on suffering. But the problem was that it set up a false belief that real life was the same. We gambled on the fact that if we played our cards right, we would pull through without too much trouble. Like Monopoly, we might even draw the "get out of jail free" card.

But real life is not like Monopoly, or even the game of Life. We do not score extra turns or cards that save the day. We do not spin the wheel of Life and get twins without the pain of delivery. But we hope that life turns out that way. We might even gamble that it does.

I believed that if I had endured one bout of suffering, then my family got a pass on going through anything else for at least ten years or more. Although it was a blatantly wrong belief, I still bought into the idea that we had time before the next bad thing would happen. Surely, nobody was like Job, experiencing one bad thing after another.

The biggest problem with this belief is that it leads us to equate having a problem-free life with God's love. When we experience trouble, we mistakenly believe that God no longer loves us. We buy into this lie because we like the idea that love and blessing are tied together and that if we are loved, then no bad things will happen to us.

No Sunday school teaching told me this. If I had really thought about his story, it would have taught me the lesson I was no better than Job. He was a good man, loved by God, and was still overwhelmed with troubles. This could happen to any of us. But no one wants to live fearing when the other shoe will drop.

Before we adopted our second child, I prayed the universal prayer of all mothers-to-be: "Please God, let the baby be healthy."

It was like praying for safe travels or a blessing over our lives. It seemed safe to ask for this blanket of protection after everything we had been through. Our adoption process took longer this time, but we knew that wasn't unusual. Once we had gotten past the hurdle of cancer, our first adoption had gone remarkably quick. Adoption was never predictable, so we held on to the belief that since this was our second time, everything would eventually work out.

After months of waiting, we finally were matched with a birth mother and a date was set for her to be induced. When Silas was born, I was present in the delivery room, witnessing the beauty of him entering our lives in a final dramatic push. As a wailing, wrinkled newborn, he protested against the shock of this cold, strange world, but quickly settled down in my arms. We swaddled him in a blanket like a burrito, and placed an ill-fitting hat from the hospital on his bald head.

Like most new moms, I spent the first several months of Silas' life smelling like spit-up and baby shampoo, enjoying those early weeks of living in the haze of sleep deprivation and baby bliss. As he grew, we began to see his easygoing nature emerge. He rarely complained and began to laugh at his sister's antics, especially when she squeezed the ranch dressing bottle and it made a farting sound.

But at his six-month checkup, we noticed a slightly concerning development. While his peers had mastered sitting up and were starting to crawl, Silas was still struggling to maintain his balance.

"Just work with him a little more," the doctor said. "We'll see how he's doing at his next appointment."

At his nine-month checkup, Silas was missing even more milestones.

His body teetered when he sat on the floor. He was like a precariously stacked tower of blocks—almost strong enough to sit, but not quite. His body flopped over and he strained to roll.

The doctor looked at him and said, "I'd like to get an MRI done to see what's going on."

"What do you think is wrong?" I asked.

"It might be something minor, like cerebral palsy," she said.

I began to cry. "I'm sorry, I'm just worried something is wrong," I choked.

I wanted my son to be healthy, the thing that every mother prays before her child is born. I didn't want him to be sick in the hospital or end up in a wheelchair. I knew what the land of the sick looked like. I had visited that place before and I did not want to go back.

"Please God, let my son be okay," I pleaded. "Please let it be something curable."

During the MRI, they sedated him and then pushed his body into a giant cavernous rocket ship where his tiny toes stuck out from a paper blanket. He looked so small beneath the giant machine that pinged and clanged.

In the past three months, we sold our home and were in the process of packing everything we owned. We left the hospital hoping nothing would come from the brain images and we could get past this little bump in the road.

But when the phone rang a few hours later and I heard the doctor's voice on the other end, I knew it was not good news. After Sam's cancer, I'd learned that most doctors don't call if the test result is normal. I closed the door of my bedroom, sat on the edge of the bed, and listened to the doctor tell me that there were dark spots on Silas' brain. I didn't understand what this meant, but I knew the doctor's words about "dying tissue on his brain" could not be good. These black spots, according to the doctor, were consistent with Leigh's disease.

The doctor had never seen a patient with it before and didn't know any details. She recommended we see a pediatric neurologist for a confirmation of the diagnosis. Since we were getting ready to close on our home, the timing couldn't have been worse.

I hung up and looked up Leigh's disease online where I learned it was a rare genetic disease that affected the brain. Then I read, "There is no cure. Life expectancy: two or three years." A wave of panic, like the kind that descends the moment before you vomit, overwhelmed me.

Over the next few days, I cried as we packed the last boxes. It was like something broke within me and I didn't know how to shut it off.

"You need to pull yourself together," Sam told me, "at least for the kids."

"I can't stop crying," I replied. "Because every time I try, I remember Silas is not going to live."

Eliana said, "It's okay Mama, it's not like Silas is going to die."

Except that he is. And I can't tell her that.

The next day, we went to the neurologist's appointment, the same day as our house closing. I hoped the diagnosis was wrong, that there was a mistake in reading the MRI and the doctor would proclaim that it was not Leigh's disease.

The doctor greeted us and then explained he needed to take a look at the images in another room. As the minutes slowly ticked by, the doctor finally returned and confirmed my worst fears: "Yes, it's Leigh's disease."

My heart dropped into my stomach. The doctor saw my face and realized he had just given me devastating news. Then he smiled and said, "Stay strong, Mama," and walked out of the room.

Stay strong? You just gave my son a death sentence and you want me to cheer up and pretend like nothing is wrong?

We left the doctor's office and went to our home closing to sign papers. What should have been a happy day of buying a new home was tainted by the doctor's confirmation of the disease. Though my mind was in a fog, I scribbled my signature on each paper, unaware of what I was even signing my name to. What did it matter anyway? I could not get the thought out of my head: *My son is dying.*

In that moment, I could only think about the little boy I loved so much and the uncertain future before us. This was the beginning of the tears. The beginning of wishing life was somehow different, that my child was healthy, that we were just a normal family, that I could go back to life before the diagnosis. This was the beginning of my begging, my pleading at the feet of God, "Please God, don't let my child die."

Yet God didn't choose us for that. He chose us to parent a broken child, to struggle through the heartache and the loss. He chose us for something I didn't feel qualified for or strong enough to endure.

My hopes for my son, everything I held onto, all of it was being burned to the ground. Yet God's promise was there, even in the black dust: he gives us "beauty instead of ashes."

How would my son's life, my life even, be turned from ashes into beauty? I could not understand it. But I held his promises close to my heart like I held my son as he slept. He would help me mother a broken child. I could embrace the brokenness of this life and somehow make it beautiful. Somehow.

EIGHT

Wanting What You Cannot Have

n the beginning, Silas looked the same as any rosy-cheeked baby with soft curls and wide eyes. Contrary to what doctors said, I looked for some sign that my son would not suffer from a terminal disease and that he would experience a normal boyhood, riding bikes and climbing trees. But even while I held out hope, I dreaded the not-too-far-away future when people would stare, or worse, look away, because it pained them to see a child so sick and broken. That day was coming, but for now, people still marveled over his beautiful hazel eyes without seeing the brokenness behind them.

Leigh's disease, from a medical standpoint, is a progressive mito-chondrial disorder that usually affects children under the age of two. The progression of the disease begins with the loss of some basic skills—sucking a bottle, unsteady head control, or sitting up. As the disease progresses, the child continues his backward slide, losing basic abilities like eating, walking, talking, and suffering from heart, vision, and breathing problems.

The disease is typically inherited from the mother and many of the cases are the result of mutations of the mitochondrial DNA. Mito-chondria are found in large numbers in most cells, and are responsible for the processes of respiration and energy production. In other words, without the mitochondria, humans would not have energy for their organs to function.

Because the disease is genetic, there is no medicine, no surgery, no treatment, absolutely nothing that could halt the progression or cure the patient. The child slowly regresses in his health, developing devas-tating problems that snowball into something catastrophic.

On a warm fall day, I put Silas down for a nap. While he was sleeping, I noticed him making a strange noise. I picked up the video monitor to see what was happening, and there was my son, stretched out in a deep sleep, making an odd guttural sound, while moving his arm in repetition with the grunt. The noise came again and again, at regular intervals. He jerked at every squeal, like someone was touching him with an electrical shock.

I snuck into his room, but I was too late. As quickly as it started, it faded away. Days passed and there were no more strange sounds on the monitor. I let the incident go until one day, I heard the bizarre noise again. I hurried into his room and watched, as his arm jerked unnaturally with a rhythmic squeal, as if someone were jerking it up, like a puppet. The noise and movement worked in tandem, but Silas did not stir.

I walked out of the room, disturbed by what I saw. Silas could potentially develop seizures with Leigh's disease, but this didn't look like epilepsy. I began putting random search words into my computer and watched videos of kids with different diseases and how their illnesses made them move in abnormal ways. I discovered there were various seizures with specific telltale signs—staring seizures, seizures that looked like hand tremors, and the dreaded grand mal seizure, where every part of the body is wracked with convulsions. Then I stumbled upon something strangely familiar, a rare kind of seizure where a child jerked one part of their body repeatedly with a curious sound. It was an unusual form of epilepsy called infantile spasms.

Seizure medications might help diminish the epilepsy, but the amount of prescribed medication could only be determined after a neurologist studied a child's EEG. The doctor wanted to see him the next time he had seizures, so they could perform the test and prescribe medication as soon as possible.

For the next few months, I watched for the seizures, but didn't see the familiar jerk or hear the strange, throaty noise. It wasn't until Sam was gone on a church staff retreat that I heard an abnormal grunt and looked over to see Silas' body wracked by convulsions. I dropped everything, put Silas in the car, and drove to the children's hospital two-and-a-half hours away.

When I arrived, the doctor told me they wanted to do an EEG test overnight so they could record electrical activity in his brain and see any seizures while he slept. I hadn't been prepared for an overnight trip and had nothing with me, but I knew we had to stay. Silas needed medication. If we waited any longer, he could die from a prolonged seizure.

They took Silas to a room where they covered his scalp in small metal discs with thin wires. To keep him from pulling off the electrodes, they wrapped his head in a cloth tube that resembled a stocking hat with a hole at the top where the wires sprouted like a ponytail. He looked like something out of an alien movie.

Since we needed to stay overnight, we were escorted to a small hospital room where another family was staying with their toddler. I called Sam to tell him about our overnight plans at the hospital and that everything would be okay.

"Are you sure I shouldn't come there?" he asked.

This would involve renting a car, and making the long trip from another state to the children's hospital, where we'd be leaving the next day.

"No, we'll be fine," I said trying to sound upbeat. "There is nothing you could do if you were here. Plus, there's not really room for another chair." I looked around our already cramped room. There was one chair on our side of the room, which would be my bed for the night.

Splitting up the family this way would become our new normal. I would learn the layout of the hospital, how to get to the cafeteria, and where the nearest snack stations were. The children's hospital was its own microcosm of activity, a home away from home for families caring for their sick children.

Silas was given a crib and my chair-bed was wedged between his crib and the privacy curtain that separated the room down the middle, splitting it into two tiny halves. To make matters worse, the chair was so small I couldn't turn around without falling off. When I tried to fall asleep that night, I realized I was lying right next to the adjoining child's father, who was sleeping in his chair on the other side of the curtain.

The next morning I woke up sore and exhausted from a restless night. Nobody warned me how poorly I would sleep in a hospital, especially with the constant stream of nurses coming in all night to check vitals. Remarkably, Silas slept better than I did. He didn't pull the wires off his head, and unlike me, managed to sleep well with the beeping machines and constant interruptions. I was not only learning hospital culture, but how to survive as a mother parenting a sick child. I slept in the clothes I had been wearing the day before and the nurses managed to find me a toothbrush. I felt like a refugee finding my way in a foreign world.

Besides the miserable sleeping quarters, I was quickly realizing that the hospital was a lonely place. What I wanted in this mess was a familiar face. I wanted home and my family. In the midst of beeping machines, it was hard to remember that God was here too, in the middle of our hospital room, holding us through the long darkness.

The family next to me was stirring as a doctor came in to check their daughter, who had fallen out of a grocery cart and gotten a concussion. From the other side of the curtain, I heard the doctor announce the good news: "You can go home today."

As they packed their stuff, I waited on some update that we'd get to leave too. My son played in his crib, his head covered in alien wires. As the family next to me prepared to leave, the mood shifted in the room. They could return to normal life and forget about this horrible night, but this was only the beginning of disrupted plans for our family. Their nightmare had been temporary, a small bump in the road that they would recount when their daughter was older. Perhaps someday, they would laugh about it as they told the story at her graduation party.

"Remember when she fell out of that cart?" they would say as they smiled and brushed off the memory like a pesky fly. They had escaped the worst. They were the lucky ones.

The stark contrast between their situation and mine couldn't be more apparent. They could forget all about what happened and go back to ordinary life, while normal life slipped between my fingers like water. Our new normal was beginning to take shape—the hospital stays, learning complex medical equipment, dealing with the stress of seizures and sickness and no answers. We would never go back to normal again, while this family was granted a reprieve.

In a strange way, I wished for what they had, even though that, too, had its own risks. I wanted the chance to choose a temporary scare over a fatal illness, but neither one of us was given that path. We could not choose. My son's story was written before he was born and his journey on earth was in a broken, failing body. My journey was to love him as he was and to keep him alive as long as we could. It would take everything I had, and even what I did not have.

As I watched the family leave the hospital and the room was finally quiet and empty, I became aware that this journey was a marathon I was not trained for.

How will I get through this? I wondered. And even more terrible: *How will I go on living when Silas does not?*

NINE

You Are Not Alone

W hen the results came back from the EEG, the doctor confirmed my internet search was correct. He had a type of seizure called infantile spasms. The treatment, unfortunately, was not easy. The miracle drug considered most effective against infantile spasms was called Acthar gel. It also happened to be wildly expensive, with each vial costing about the price of our minivan. Although the medicine was only used for a short amount of time to eliminate the seizures, Silas would need several vials and the cost of treatment would run about the same as purchasing a house, around $100,000 or more. Insurance would not cover it.

We were told that the National Organization for Rare Disorders program would likely pay for the drug if we were willing to apply. But like everything, it was a gamble. If insurance wouldn't cover it and neither did this organization, we would be stuck footing a $100,000 bill. It was considered the most effective drug against this type of seizure, which was crucial to bring under control because of the devastating effects on the brain. We were desperate and agreed to the plan, knowing we were gambling everything we owned on this miracle drug. The drug could only be administered through a needle, which meant that we needed to learn how to perform injections.

"We will teach you how to do that," they told us at the doctor's office as if it were no big deal. If there's one thing I've always hated, it was needles, and now here I was, learning how to use one on my son. The nurse showed us how to prepare the drug, prep the needle, and insert it in his thigh. I breathed deep and willed myself not to faint.

It was never discussed whether we *could* do it. We would learn to inject this drug into our squirming son's thigh while he screamed in pain, because our son needed the medicine. Forget the fact that we had no medical training and no knowledge. This seemed as absurd to me as learning to fly the space shuttle.

When we started this journey through Leigh's disease, I assumed that health professionals, who had training and education, would administer all the medical care, while I would comfort my child. But that was only partially true. There were, of course, certain tasks left to doctors and nurses, but I was quickly learning that more would be required of me than I thought possible.

We learned from the doctor that the drug would make him puffy and fat, like a slowly expanding balloon. It also came with a host of dangerous side effects, and most frightening, no guarantee that it would work. For some kids, it was a miracle drug, stopping the seizures altogether. For others, it temporarily halted the epilepsy, but over time, the seizures returned once the treatment was weaned. We knew the cure came at a heavy cost. With the stress of injecting it daily and the hefty price tag, the emotional toll seemed worse than the drug. As we faced a grim reality, we were desperate to try the drug, risks and all.

A few days later, we got the phone call. We had been accepted into the program that paid for the drug. Despite the outrageous cost, a deliveryman brought it to our front porch like a mail package. I found it sitting outside, shipped on dry ice to keep the vials cold. I placed the costly medicine inside our fridge next to Tupperware leftovers and condiments, and then opened another box that contained the needles. Our family now owned boxes of drug paraphernalia. Even the words made me feel like a criminal.

Piles of syringes and needles graced my counters. *Where in the world am I going to put these?* Normal people don't have a dedicated space for medical supplies and Googling "where do I store my needles?" probably wouldn't give me the answer I needed either. I doubted that illegal drug users really bothered to worry about where they stored their needles.

I decided to rearrange our bathroom closet and put it on a high shelf where it would be out of the way. I didn't want to see it, even if that meant pretending we were a normal family with sippy cups on our shelves instead of syringes.

I realized with horror that the arrival of the medication also meant that we needed to start injections that night. I thought of the game Operation and how as a child, my hand had shaken violently when I tried to remove the funny bone. The more I focused on not shaking, the worse it got, and soon the buzzer roared furiously, which made my hand jump even more.

That night after dinner, Silas lay on the floor while I reviewed the procedures for the injection. We decided that Sam would stick him with the needle, while I held him still.

"We need to distract him," I said. "Why don't we sing a song?"

Everyone agreed to sing "Jesus Loves Me" as Silas looked obliviously unaware of what was about to happen. Eliana sat near his head and I held his legs so he wouldn't kick the needle. As a family, we were going to do this together, no matter how hard.

"Let's get this over with," Sam said, his face grave.

When it came to doing something he hated, he just put his head down and plowed through it. There was no hesitation. No questioning whether he would do it right. There was only finishing the job. I had always loved this trait about him, but I never imagined a scenario like this.

I grabbed Silas' legs and held them firmly. Then we began to sing, "Jesus loves me this I know, for the Bible tells me so."

Sam pushed the needle deeper into Silas' thigh as our singing grew louder.

"Little ones to him belong."

Silas paused, bewildered by what was happening, then began to cry as Sam pulled the needle out of his leg.

"They are weak, but he is strong!"

Silas wailed furiously while I slapped a bandage on him and cradled him in my arms. As he cried, I held him tight, feeling the tears sting my eyes. There was nothing we could do to explain that this pain we were causing him was actually our best attempt to heal him. The task I had dreaded all day was done. Then I realized, with horror, that we would have to do it again tomorrow and the next day.

For the next few weeks, we managed to get through the daily injections. While it still remained a dreaded part of our day, we knew we were one day closer to finishing treatment. His seizures were decreasing and then one day, they disappeared. The medicine was working.

During that time, I found an online medical board for parents who had children with infantile spasms. One of the women happened to mention she was living in the same town as I was. Her son, who was around the same age as Silas, was going through the same treatment. It seemed too coincidental to ignore.

I reached out to her and mentioned I was from the same city. She immediately responded with such warmth that I asked if she wanted to meet and invited her over to my house. I've never been the type of person who extended an invitation before even meeting a person, but something felt right about her.

When Jewels arrived at my home, she immediately smiled and made me feel at ease. We put our kids on the floor together and sat down next to them, like moms on a playdate. Instead of talking about normal baby stuff, we discussed everything seizure-related: infantile spasms, the horribly expensive medication, our fear of the future. Finally, I had found someone who understood how bewildering this journey was.

For the first time, a friend understood the stress of epilepsy, the pain of injecting your screaming child, and the fragile hope that they might be healed. Like me, she mourned the loss of having a child who might not have a normal childhood.

Before I met Jewels, I thought I was the only one. But the beauty of friendship was discovering that we were not alone. We had stumbled across each other online, not realizing that we lived only fifteen minutes apart. After meeting, I realized she filled that void of understanding that other friends could not.

As she left that day, her son in her arms, I was reminded that no matter how alone I felt, other moms were wading through the journey with me, offering their hands in the dark. And somehow, we would get through it together.

TEN

Not What I Signed Up for

○———————————————————○

The drug was working wonders on our son, but a child could not be on it indefinitely. It was only a temporary drug, with the hope that if we slowly weaned him off, the seizures would not return. But the weaning process had complications. Children taken off the drug often lost their appetite and their thirst for liquids, which put them at risk for dehydration. When we began the weaning process, hopeful the drug would continue working, our son started refusing all food and drinks.

"Here Silas, you need to drink something," I begged at the dining room table, holding his bottle.

He turned his face away from the drink and clenched his teeth. When I tried to insert the bottle in his mouth, the milk seeped out the sides of his lips. His appetite had bottomed out and no matter what we tried—fruit juice, popsicles, sweetened drinks, he refused it. His aversion to food could not even be swayed by the most tempting syrupy sweet soda. If we didn't find something soon, he would end up in the hospital.

I mixed up two bowls of applesauce and orange juice and I took a tiny spoonful and wriggled it into his mouth. Since he did not spit it out, I scooped up another spoonful, quick to capitalize on this small success. We had finally found something he would eat, even if he was only eating one bite at a time. Day after day, I fed him applesauce and orange juice from a spoon. The tediousness of feeding him all his liquids by the spoonful meant we spent hours at the table, but somehow, we kept him out of the hospital. This was a small victory, but I was counting every one.

One day out of the corner of my eye, I saw Silas' arm jerk in a strange way. After all the injections and side effects, the seizures had returned. They continued to multiply as the drug slowly worked its way out of his system. He had seizures when we were shopping, seizures when the temperature was too hot or cold, seizures at night, and seizures in the car while I was driving. This happened so often when I was alone with the kids, I learned how to drive with one hand, while simultaneously reaching for my son in the backseat to help him.

Not only did he have seizures nearly everywhere we went, he also developed different types of seizures—something I was oblivious to before entering the epilepsy world. When my son had his first grand mal seizure, he was taking a midday nap. Just like his first seizure, I heard a strange sound on the video monitor and then saw his body shaking. When I rushed into his room, he was convulsing furiously and his face looked contorted with fear.

"It's okay Silas, Mama is here!" I shouted, but he did not hear me. His eyes were wide with terror, while the convulsions wracked his body. Then as quickly as it appeared, it disappeared and he fell back exhausted. I picked him up and held him tightly to my chest. As I cradled his weak body in my arms, I cried knowing there was nothing I could do to stop the seizures.

There were a lot of bad things about this disease—the way he was losing his strength, his ability to swallow, even his smile. But of all the things I hated about my son's disease, the seizures were the worst. I knew this disease was no surprise for God, but it had been for me, and I struggled with understanding why my son had been chosen. The ugly truth was I wanted my son to be normal and he was not.

Sitting in the waiting room of the children's hospital during another routine appointment, I looked around at the parents who, like me, didn't sign up for this gig. Not one of us would have chosen to be a parent of a special needs child, given the chance. We would have gladly taken our child, free from medical conditions, and bowed out from this medical journey. We would have jumped at the chance for the same child with normal health and abilities. But we weren't given that option. So here we were, waiting for our ten minutes with a doctor who would only have answers that were, at best, Band-Aids for a devastating and gaping wound.

I used to believe that being a parent to a special needs child was reserved for people who had some unique quality, like an abundance of mercy or an extra dose of patience. Little did I know no one ever sees herself destined to parent a terminally ill child. When it happens, you're suddenly thrust into a club you didn't ask to join. It seemed there must be some mistake. Certainly, God chose the wrong person.

Most days, I struggled with managing the little things, like relearning how to do everyday tasks with a fragile child. Because of his very low muscle tone, Silas struggled to sit in a grocery cart, couldn't eat normal food in restaurants, and had seizures in public. He needed medications throughout the day, some which required being crushed and added to liquids. He was fed with a feeding tube and machine. This wasn't exactly convenient if you were out running errands. His body couldn't handle summer heat or winter cold because it caused more seizures, so spending time outside was difficult.

Even going to the store was a challenge. At first, I pretended that I was just like the other moms at Target, hauling around their preschoolers, while picking up baby wipes and toothpaste. Even though Silas could not sit up in a traditional cart, we found a special two-seat cart for toddlers that had a taller back to support bigger kids. Eliana sat in one seat and I strapped Silas in the other, tightening the shoulder straps so he could sit up and rest his head against the back of the molded plastic. He still struggled to hold his head, but this was the best option we had, and I was determined to be like the other moms who shopped with their kids.

As we waited at the checkout, I noticed something from my cart was dripping onto the floor. Silas slumped against the seatbelts, which were holding him up like a rag doll. I peeked a glance at the cart again, noticing we were leaving wet spots across the floor.

I tried to hide my panic as I loaded bags into my cart and paid the bill. My first instinct was to get him out of the store as quickly as possible to see where the mysterious dripping was coming from. As I left, a trail of drops followed me across the tile floor.

When we got to the car, I stopped the cart, unbuckled my son, and discovered to my horror, that not only was his diaper leaking, but he had experienced a major blowout. It was every parent's nightmare—being in a public place with a child who had diarrhea *everywhere*. Due to his medical condition and weak muscles, he had regular struggles with constipation. Because he was now on a special ketogenic diet for seizures, he could not have fruit or juice to help the problem like before. The only solution was a laxative, but sometimes he was so backed up, the product worked too well and it all came out in one giant explosion. Worst of all, I never knew when these explosions were due to arrive. We would wait days and suddenly all the you-know-what hit the fan. Except in this case, it was the Target cart.

At that point, I had a major dilemma. I could attempt to change his diarrhea-soaked clothes in a public restroom or I could just wipe up the mess, put him in the car and deal with the problem when I got home. Although both options were far from ideal, I knew it would be easier to deal with the mess at home where I could bathe him, wash the car seat, and drop his clothes directly in the washing machine.

After that unfortunate ordeal, I stopped taking my son to the store with me. It wasn't just because of the massive diaper explosion. As the complications of his health grew, I couldn't carry all his medical equipment with me. Then there were the practical issues. Because he had no head or muscle control, he was getting too big for me to carry and could not sit on my hip like a toddler. The seat belts on most carts no longer fit him and it was impossible for me to push a wheelchair and a cart at the same time.

I could no longer pretend to be a normal mom taking my kids to the grocery store. This was something hard to give up—the word *normal* and everything that meant to me. I wanted to be a normal wife, parenting two normal kids, and living a normal life. But normal life, though in itself not a bad thing, can become an idol too. It can be something we constantly strive for, when what we've been given is a very extraordinary life that is anything but normal.

Before Silas was born, I prayed for a healthy child. I thought that God would only give a very fragile little boy to someone well-equipped to handle the demands of a sick child. In other words, *not me*. But instead, God chose us, a family who had no experience with a special needs child.

There can be a huge chasm between the life we imagine for our-selves and what actually happens. Try as I might, I could not change the fact that my son was very sick. Even when his body stiffened in seizures or when his head flopped forward because he no longer had the strength to hold it up, I knew he was made in God's image and experienced his love. I saw it, each night at dinner, when we pulled out a worn, yellowed copy of a children's Bible I had growing up. When we read the story, Silas tried to lift his head to look at the pictures. It was, some days, the only life we would see in his face.

Silas reminded us that inside this broken body was a little boy who could not get out, but whose life emerged in the smallest of ways—head turned toward the book, eyes flickering some recognition, lips curled in the tiniest of smiles. He was made in God's image too. In the midst of all the hard stuff—the late nights cleaning up a feeding tube that leaked all over the bed or watching our boy's body wracked by a half-dozen seizures—there was still some beauty in the brokenness. Disease stripped Silas of a normal childhood of climbing rocks, run-ning down sidewalks, and riding bikes, but it could not take away the image of God in him.

When I was in college, we performed a dramatic sketch called "Crooked Town." In the story, the characters were bent into funny angles, but didn't realize this, because they couldn't see how crooked they were. Everyone was broken and blind to their own bent-out-of-shape bodies. Eventually, a character arrived in the story who was able to undo all the crookedness and the people suddenly straightened up—no more hunched-over bodies. Before, they could not see their crookedness because everybody was crooked, but once they were healed, they realized how bent they had been.

Years later, I looked at my son, and his broken, crooked body. He was hunched over, his head tilted unnaturally to the side, and his joints contorted into strange, stiffened movements. Even with his imperfections, we could still see the image of God in him.

He was broken, and yet so beautiful, and one day, all that brokenness would be healed. In this tension, we learned to struggle through what we thought our lives would look like, and accept what they really were. Through it all, we longed for the healing that was yet to be.

ELEVEN

He Is Not Silent

My life was split between home and the hospital. Everything else that didn't involve Silas' health had to be stripped away so that we could be united in one goal: keeping our son alive. I didn't know it would take all of me, but I didn't care how much it cost either. Every time I looked into my little boy's eyes, I knew why it had to be done. We wanted a little more time with him.

Every morning, I woke up and checked Silas' G-tube and the feeding machine that pumped his formula into his stomach. I measured out a long list of medications, and then prepped the pills, cutting and crushing the pills into dust, then mixing it all into his formula.

We did this several times a day, in between his daily schedule of medical appointments, which included physical, occupational and speech therapists, and appointments with at least four specialists. On a regular basis, I struggled with juggling all these roles, so I dropped out of everything else—playdates, social activities, ministry opportunities, part-time work, volunteering, even writing.

I fell into bed at night exhausted, and then woke up several times a night to check on him, to make sure his feeding machine was working and his breathing was normal. When I'd peek in his room, his little pink cheek was pressed into the mattress, his body turned toward his Woody doll, while his limp hand grasped for his stuffed friend.

This was how our days rolled into one another. My mind was constantly thinking of what Silas needed next—prescription refills, medical equipment, another doctor's appointment. When we left the house, it was like moving a small city. We had to load the wheelchair in the car, medical supplies, and what seemed like a million other things, just in case.

At that time, we were on a waiting list to receive nursing care through the state, which would provide at least an hour break every week. Granted, it was only an hour, but it meant I would have help. The only downside was that because it was a government program, and there were so many families in need of these services, I was told we would need to wait seven years before we would receive these services. The waiting list was extremely long, but each day was a day closer to getting to the front of the line.

One day, I got a call from this state program. "Due to some changes in the program," the worker explained, "we decided that kids two and under will not qualify for these services anymore. Because of that, we are taking you off the waiting list. You can reapply when your son is older and start over on the waiting list at that time."

My mind was still processing what she just said. *We are being taken off the waiting list. We need to start all over again.*

"Wait, why is this being changed?" I asked the lady on the other end.

"The qualifications we use to judge whether a child needs our services don't apply to a two-year-old," she explained. "We look at things like whether they can comb their hair or not, or eat without help. A toddler can't comb their hair. They can't use a fork. They can't do much independently, so they don't qualify for our services now."

I heard her talking, but I was throbbing with anger. *My son cannot even hold up his head. He has a G-tube because he chokes on food. I suction his mouth so he doesn't aspirate his saliva. How can you say he is no different from any other child?* Every day I was reminded that the gulf between my child and other children his age was widening.

I tried to keep my voice from shaking as I explained, "My son cannot even sit by himself, hold his head up, or eat regular food. How can you say that he doesn't need help?"

"I'm sorry," the lady said. "Our waiting list is so long. I think this was a way to reduce the number of children on it."

There it was. The *real* reason. They needed a way to cut down their waiting list so they just lopped off all of the youngest kids. Instead of redoing the qualifications based on the severity of the illness, they based it on age. Instead of writing up qualifications that would help the children who were the sickest, they made a hasty decision that left our family, and many others, without services. Now they were taking us off the list, and we would have to start all over on the seven-year wait.

That's when the realization hit me: my son would never get these services. Even if he went back on the list, by the time he made it to the front of the line, he most likely wouldn't even be alive.

My voice cracked as I said goodbye and hung up. I stood at the window and looked out. The world outside my house, a lush green, tree-lined street, looked like some place unreachable, like a world I could only see, but never touch.

God, I need help, I prayed. *I am so tired.*

God already knew how tired I was, but it lifted a load off to tell him this, just like when I met with friends for coffee and shared my struggles. Confessing the truth made me feel better, even when there were no answers.

I didn't know how help would come, or whether it would come at all, but I'd learned in the worst of situations, when I sunk to my lowest point, that turning to God and asking for what seemed impossible was the only hope I had left. I was at a point where I could not make the situation, nor my son, better. I didn't even know how we'd get through next week, let alone the next few years. But praying at a window, tears streaming down my face, was the only thing I knew how to do.

A few weeks later, Sam was approached by a couple after church. The wife told Sam that she woke up in the middle of the night with the sense she should pray for us. While she was praying, she sensed that God was leading her to ask whether she could help us. She wondered if she and her husband might learn how to take care of Silas, so that I could enjoy a break every once in a while.

When Sam told me this, he hadn't known about my prayer at the

window. It was a conversation between me and God, a private pleading, and I knew that telling him I needed more help would just make
him feel guilty. He tried to provide breaks for me as much as he could,
but he also had a full-time ministry job as a worship pastor. He juggled
his own demands and then came home and started his second job as
dad, husband, and caregiver.

"Yes," I told him. "Tell her yes."

It's one thing to say God answered prayer, but it's a whole other
thing to experience an answer to prayer that was so crystal clear. In
that moment, I realized I was not forgotten. God cared about the small
things in my life. He not only provided me with someone to give me
a break, but he showed me an example of someone who prayed and
responded. If she had gone back to sleep, or just ignored it, would I
ever have known God's loving care through this situation? Would he
have sent someone else?

That situation taught me two important lessons. First, in my weak-
est moment, God will provide what I need. When I cried out in prayer
for help, God didn't leave me to figure out a solution. He wasn't silent.
Crying out for help was a good prayer when I didn't know what else
to say.

Second, I needed to listen and respond to what God was asking
of me. So often, I second-guessed what God was leading me to do.
I wondered, *Did you really want me to do this? Did I hear you right?* But in
this situation, help appeared because someone listened and followed
through. I didn't have to know all the answers to how I would do something, I just needed to take the first step of faith and act.

This was my answer to prayer, and for the first time in a long time,
things finally were going smoothly.

TWELVE

The Beginning of the End

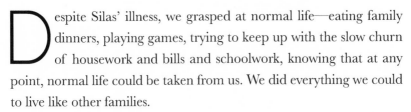

Despite Silas' illness, we grasped at normal life—eating family dinners, playing games, trying to keep up with the slow churn of housework and bills and schoolwork, knowing that at any point, normal life could be taken from us. We did everything we could to live like other families.

"Normal life is underrated," my husband said to me one day. "People don't realize how great it is until it's gone."

One day, I came across a TV show that showed how dogs could help people with disabilities. The dogs, who had gone through extensive training, learned how to turn on and off light switches, open doors, and were even trained to identify when a seizure was coming on.

I started checking into therapy centers where dogs were trained to prepare for their specific role. The cost was steep, and Silas' young age and inability to communicate prevented us from qualifying. Even though we couldn't have a therapy dog, that didn't disqualify us from getting a regular dog.

For some time, I had tried to think of ways my son could have friends. He was not invited on playdates because he was too fragile and at risk for health complications if he got sick. My son's only friends were the three therapists that came to work with him—his speech, occupational, and physical therapist that stopped by once a week. Because he spent so much time with us, I wanted him to have a companion that could give him some sense of a normal life.

After doing some research, we decided that a golden retriever would be the best choice, since Silas could pet her from his wheelchair. A few months later, our home was invaded by a rambunctious six-month-old golden doodle named Allie. Silas perked up when he saw her, his big eyes watching her pace the floor. One night, when we were eating on the patio, he saw Allie walk by his wheelchair and his face broke into a grin. It was the first smile we had seen in months.

Allie was a bright spot in our lives, always greeting us at the door and jumping on us to demonstrate how thrilled she was to see our faces. Like most puppies, she managed to chew all the toys within reach of her teeth. Barbies with mangled limbs dotted the house. Stuffed animals were ripped apart, their pieces scattered across the family room. When we took them away, she looked ashamed, but within a few hours, she was back to foraging the toy box. Her ears perked up whenever we mentioned a walk or pulled out a ball for fetch.

Her puppy exuberance was a welcome change amidst Silas' declining health. After picking up a virus, Silas developed a swollen lymph node that would not heal, despite trying multiple rounds of antibiotics. The doctor examined the angry red bump on his neck and determined that the best thing would be to remove it. Surgery was not ideal for Silas—his Leigh's disease always worsened when he was under stress, wreaking havoc on his body. But we also could not leave a raging infection in his body.

The nurse took a sharpie and circled the huge lymph node under his jawbone, and then wrote in big letters next to it, "Yes." This would help the surgeon to avoid taking out the wrong one, even though it seemed obvious since it was a screaming red lump.

We both kissed Silas and then left our son with the nurse who was wheeling him into the operating room. Panic rose up in my chest. *What if Silas dies in surgery? What if this is my last goodbye?*

Silas was fragile in a way that other children were not. He had a long list of restrictions in the hospital, even on the type of IV fluid he could receive. His body had weakened so much that when I picked him up, he sagged like a sack of potatoes in my arms. He could not hold up his head for more than a few seconds, despite his weekly physical therapy. He choked on his saliva and turned blue when he coughed. He was almost three years old, yet he was as weak as a newborn. He struggled through a half dozen seizures daily that continued to drag him in a downward spiral. It seemed to pull all of us with him, even while we fought for a miracle.

A few hours later, they led us to his bedside where he lay sleeping, still groggy from the anesthesia. When Sam said his name, he opened his eyes slowly and gave him a look that said, *I'm so happy to see you.* He could no longer smile, but occasionally, we saw a spark of something in his eyes and the slightest upturn of his tiny pink lips, and we knew that this was joy. We held on to those small moments like precious gifts, even though they were slowly slipping from our hands like sand, as he spiraled toward an inevitable descent we could not stop.

Over the next few months, we noticed Silas was losing everything—his smile, head control, and the ability to stay awake for more than a few hours—and the doctors started offering fewer answers. Silas was pummeled by seizures multiple times a day and had failed so many medications we were running out of options. We had reached a turning point where medical science no longer could guide us.

I researched experimental drugs and prayed for healing, even though we were not seeing improvement. I sat in waiting rooms expecting doctors to have answers and stroked his skin while he slept in hospital beds, hoping for a miracle. I worked his legs and arms through physical therapy exercises, thinking if he could get stronger, then his health would improve. But he continued to weaken, like a fading flower that slowly wilts in the noonday sun. I prayed through hot tears. I begged God for help. As I waited, all I heard was silence. Somehow, I held on to who God was, despite the fact my prayers were not being answered the way I wanted. Even though I knew God had ordained Silas' days, I did not want to imagine the worst or how I would live through it.

Many years before, I knew a man who said he stopped praying after a loved one died. He felt like God had failed him in his most desperate time, when his wife had collapsed and he begged God to save her. When she passed away, he had given up believing that prayer made any difference. Like this man, I realized it was easy to believe in God when our prayers are answered, but just as tempting to doubt God's goodness when he says "no."

We are not protected from the brokenness of this world because we pray or have faith in Christ. If we were, then everyone would be praying, if only to escape the awful suffering of this world. We pray, because prayer transforms us, even when it doesn't change our situation. As I looked at my son sleeping in his wheelchair, I was afraid of the worst and I wanted him changed too.

In the fall of that year, Silas got sick with a raging ear infection. His breathing suddenly grew strained and I took him to the doctor four times in one week, where he was treated with multiple drugs to get the infection under control. After his last doctor's appointment, I checked on him again in the middle of the night, noticing his breathing had relaxed into slow, deep breaths. This seemed like good news and I crawled back into bed, relieved he finally was resting deeply.

The next morning, I woke up early to check on him, and noticed his breathing seemed slower than normal. Though dark in his room, the hall light illuminated the outline of his body. I started silently counting his breaths as I strained to see my watch.

One, two, three.

The seconds seemed to be flying by fast, while my son's breathing seemed laborious and slow.

Four, five, six. He should be breathing faster. Seven, eight, nine.

I tried to rouse him with a small shake. He didn't respond. His disease made him unusually sleepy, but rousing him would cause some kind of physiological response, like an eyelid flutter or a slight movement to show his discomfort at being wakened. This time, there was nothing.

Ten, eleven, twelve.

At nearly one minute, I realized his breathing was too slow. My sleepiness in the early morning darkness was jolted by an urgency to find help. I bolted down the hall to get Sam.

"Silas' breathing is really slow," I told Sam as a wave of panic surged up in me. "I need your help."

Sam ran past Eliana's bedroom, who was roused from sleep by our commotion. He turned on the bright light of Silas' room, something I hadn't done out of an instinct to let my child rest. I learned to check on Silas' feeding tube and breathing in the light of medical machines and nightlights so that I wouldn't wake him. But now, we needed to see exactly what was going on.

Sam lifted his fingers and looked at his fingernails. "His fingers are blue. We need to call an ambulance."

For only a second I saw his fingers, the tiny discolored nails I had failed to look at in the dark. So often I had held those fingers in mine as I helped him grasp a toy or hold a crayon. His muscles had weakened to the point where he could not hold anything, so his therapist gave me some crayons with a Velcro strap. We strapped the crayon around his palm, then I wrapped my hand around his, and let the crayon slide across the blank page. I guided his hand back and forth, then I'd let go to see if he could scribble on his own. Most of the time, his hand stopped, like a limp rag. But every once in a while, he'd fling his hand across the page, the crayon leaving one long mark of red. It wasn't much, but he'd done it himself. One beautiful, long line. Now those hands that had been so securely wrapped in mine were tinged an unnatural shade of blue.

"I need to get him out of bed," Sam said, unhooking the feeding tube from his belly, which was still pumping his formula. He picked him up and lifted him onto the floor to perform CPR as I ran down the hall to call the ambulance. Sam began pumping his chest, pleading for him to wake up.

"Come on Silas," Sam muttered in a strained voice. "Come on!"

The first person to arrive was a policewoman, who ran up the stairs and took over CPR, followed by the arrival of the ambulance crew. They were faceless men, but their boots, heavy and black, left stark imprints in the carpet of our hallway.

Eliana stood in her pajamas at her bedroom door watching it all unfold. Sam took her quickly to another room, so she would not see the paramedics working or get in their way.

"Pray for your brother," he said and left to return to Silas' side. Later when he walked by, he saw her kneeling on the floor, praying for her brother, her arms wrapped around the dog's neck in a desperate hug.

As parents, we grasp fierce hope in the most tragic of circumstances. We fight for it, hang on to every last shred, and pray for second chances. Dawn would never come that day. The dark morning would turn to grey clouds and a steady rain, foreshadowing an ending that, moments before, had seemed like a normal day.

The paramedics loaded Silas onto a stretcher and into the ambulance and told us that only one parent could ride in the ambulance, while the other could follow. I crawled into the emergency vehicle and we sped off onto rainy streets, already packed with cars on their way to work. The emergency room staff was waiting for us when we arrived and rolled the stretcher into a large room with bright lights.

"He has Leigh's disease," I told one nurse. "I have a list of medications."

They scrambled to revive him, but at some point, the action of the room suddenly slowed down, like a movie in slow motion. The room turned strangely quiet as the staff began to wander out.

What is happening?

I stood in the middle of the chaos, as nurses circled around me, avoiding my gaze. An older gentleman with a greying beard and a pale face appeared, floating and silent, like a ghost. He stood next to the wall and said nothing. No one acknowledged him. He folded his hands and gazed at my son and I realized, looking at his collar, he was the hospital chaplain.

The silent weight of the room didn't fully explain it, but the appearance of this ghost chaplain finally answered my question. *Is my son alive?* His presence told me what I did not want to know.

Sometimes the worst things of life appear at the times when we are least prepared, when we think we're safe because the danger has passed. We breathe a sigh of relief, turn to go, and get pummeled by a wave so big, our feet get knocked out from under us. Even though I knew my son would die from his disease, we saw no signs this was the end. No writing on the wall. No time to say goodbye. After the medical staff had left us alone in the emergency room, I looked at his tiny, lifeless body and everything broke inside me. Sam and I stared at our little boy and held each other as the tears streamed down our faces like the pouring rain outside.

I had no memory of the chaplain saying anything, although it's possible he did. My brain, in those early hours of my son's death, was filled with both hazy and vivid memories, blank spaces where I couldn't remember what happened and other things I'll never forget.

Sam leaned over and laid his hands on Silas' body and began to pray through his tears, "Our Father, who art in heaven, hallowed be thy name."

The chaplain, silent until now, stood on the other side of Silas and put his hands on top of Sam's and prayed with him. "Thy kingdom come. Thy will be done, on earth as it is in heaven…"

Hospital chaplains do their work in the early hours of death, when families stagger at the news of death. They've seen the elderly pass away—the grandparents and great grandparents—but when death changes the predictable order of things, when it steals young ones from their parents, there is no explanation for that, just the heaviness of a weary world that is too broken to fix.

This truth weighed on him and he could not carry it. As quickly as the chaplain drifted in, he drifted out.

Outside the rain poured like a steady lament. It felt like God was weeping with us.

THIRTEEN

The Question You Cannot Answer

Through those early weeks living in a fog of tears, we had to make countless decisions, from burial plots to funeral plans. I was not prepared for the overload, or how devastating it would be to select my child's casket. When the funeral director asked me what kind of clothes I wanted to bury Silas in, I told him I didn't know. Silas had grown recently, but I hadn't bought new clothes yet, and the dress clothes in his closet were too small. I rifled through his dresser to find an outfit, pulling out shirts and pants, but none of the clothes were nice enough for a funeral. This was the last outfit I would see him in. Somehow nothing seemed good enough. The thought of shopping for my son, to buy him dress clothes that I would never see him wear while he was alive, stung like a cruel joke.

I ended up at one of the most expensive department stores in town, looking through tiny dress suits, button-down shirts, and plaid ties. Normally I would have been gushing over these adorable clothes, but today I could only look at them sadly, and wonder why I had never shopped here when my son was alive. I knew the answer to that question, that buying an outfit off the rack here cost what I would pay for three outfits somewhere else. And yet, wasn't my son worth it? Why hadn't I done this for him, just once?

I carried my guilt like a heavy brick, a punishment for not doing enough, even though I knew I had done my best. This is one of the cruelest parts of grief, the feeling that in the end, your best was not good enough.

Walking around racks of clothes, I finally found a crisp purple dress shirt, plaid tie, dark dress pants, and a *Thomas the Train* t-shirt that he would wear underneath the dress clothes. It didn't matter that no one would see it. Silas loved Thomas, even if, on most days, holding the little engine in his weak fingers was too hard for him.

As I walked up to the counter to pay, the sales lady looked at my purchase, smiled, and said, "You must be buying this for a very special occasion."

I paused, struck by her words. *A special occasion. My son's funeral.* The words seemed sacred somehow, unbelievable even to me. I could not open my lips to tell her the truth.

"Yes," I mumbled as she folded the dress shirt with perfect precision.

The question of what the special occasion was hung in the air unanswered as she carefully placed each piece of clothing in the bag, like delicate china. I imagined the look on her face if I told her the truth, her expression crumbling into shock, the apologies pouring out.

I looked away from her face and clamped my mouth shut. *Let her imagine we are going to a special occasion—a wedding, perhaps, where all the guests would gush over this outfit.*

"Thank you," I said, grabbing my package and heading quickly out of the store.

In every life, there is a before and an after, a clear split between one chapter and another, a door we step through, while another closes and locks behinds us. I had crossed a threshold and I sensed this most in the small moments, like buying Silas' last outfit and throwing away my stolen purse. It was not supposed to be this way, but I could not go back to the way things were.

In the weeks after Silas' death, I went in his room, picked out a shirt, and smelled it, trying to remember his scent before it was gone, before the clothes picked up that stale smell of musty air.

They say some women never stop mothering their children once they are grown, but the same is true for the mothers who bury their children. We continue to imagine our babies, and how grown up they'd look, or what they'd be doing now. We think of how we would bury our noses in their hair, breathing in their intoxicating scent, and we'd give anything for one more chance to cup their faces and kiss their soft cheeks.

Once, after Silas' bath, I told my family, "I hope heaven smells like a freshly washed baby." I said it half-joking, but I do hope heaven smells like my son after a bath, with his curly hair pressed against my cheek.

When someone leaves us, we live by these fragments of memory and they remind us the person we love still has a story and their story is not done. We remember the sound of their laughter, the curl of their eyelashes, the faint smell of their skin, etched in our minds like a beautiful dream. And we remember a hazy image of someone who wrings our heart out and we grasp for them in the dark with fierce hope.

As I lay in bed, I wondered how I would go on after the worst had happened. I did not want this ending. But *it was written*—and I must find my way out of the dark.

PART TWO

After

It's okay if it feels hard.
It's okay that you don't know
the way ahead of you.
Even in the unknown,
you'll discover strength
in the darkness
that will carry you
toward the soft light
of rising hope.

FOURTEEN

Finding the Gifts of Brokenness

F or weeks, I walked around in a haze. The funeral, and all the decisions surrounding it, occurred in a blur of grief. Neighbors and church friends dropped off casseroles and baked pasta at our home. Sometimes I ate, while other times I choked food down. My body didn't feel hungry, it felt tired and heavy, like I was dragging a load of bricks.

When I fell into bed at night, I couldn't stop the flashbacks from the final week before Silas died. I was like a bird circling above the situation in an endless loop. My brain, replaying the trauma of everything that had happened, couldn't shut off this horrible nightmare.

When the alarm rang early the next morning, I rolled over, turned it off, and fell back asleep where I imagined Silas was still alive, sleeping soundly in his bedroom. It became a vicious cycle of insomnia, followed by sleeping too much. When I finally woke up, I realized Silas was gone again and I could feel a slow ache descend on me. Facing the day without him was another sort of nightmare.

"In this first year of grief, you might think you are going crazy," a pastor told me. "But it's all normal. Feeling like you are going crazy *is* normal."

Learning that "crazy was normal" helped me, but it didn't stop others from offering their well-intentioned, but typically unhelpful advice. They wanted me to move on and get back to normal, because they believed that normal meant happy. I did not even know what normal looked like anymore.

A few weeks later, when both Sam and Eliana went back to their regular routines of work and school, I found myself, without warning, alone in a quiet home that echoed with memories. I expected to walk in a room and see Silas in his wheelchair, but instead, I only found the dog lying on the floor looking up at me. We had both lost a companion.

What do we do now? her eyes seemed to say. She looked as dejected as I felt, with her chin resting on the floor and her brown eyes gazing up at me. My daily routine for the last several years revolved around taking care of Silas, but now my days swung wide open, like an ugly, giant void. Instead of a sense of possibility, a hole gaped with his absence.

As Sam was getting ready to leave for work, I told him, "I'm not sure what to do with myself."

"Take your time to heal," he responded. "You don't have to feel like you need to do anything. You'll figure out what to do."

It seemed so simple: *Figure out what to do.* But since the whiplash of change left me stunned, the last thing I could decide was what to do with my newfound freedom. *Go back to work? Knock out a home project? Pick up a new hobby?* None of it sounded appealing.

In addition, the world continued to make its demands. I stumbled through my daily tasks, clumsily trying to please everyone, while feeling like I was failing at most everything. Sometimes I left the house, but found that introduced another set of problems. On a regular basis, I ran into people who either avoided talking to me or tried to ask about my grief, but really seemed uncomfortable with the subject.

"How are you, really?" they'd ask.

I didn't know what to say because I could barely get out of bed. I wanted to tell them, "My life just hit rock bottom, how do you think I'm doing?" Instead, I replied, "Okay."

But was I okay, *really?*

After a few months of struggling through sleepless nights and taking care of all the final medical and funeral bills, I came down with a terrible flu, complete with fever, chills, and a pounding headache.

I sunk into the couch and fell into a deep, feverish sleep. Suddenly a hand tapped my shoulder and I heard my daughter's gentle plea.

"I'm hungry," she said peering over my face as I slept.

It was dinnertime and Sam wouldn't be home from work until late.

I dragged myself off the couch to the refrigerator, where I found some frozen soup, and dropped it into a pot. It hurt to stand as I turned the heat on high and stirred the frozen pieces of broth.

Even calling someone on the phone seemed overwhelming. My only goal was making the hurt stop—the pain in my body, the hurt in my heart, the broken pieces of my life.

The soup bubbled and sputtered. I poured it into a bowl, handed it to my daughter, and then collapsed on the couch, my body shaking with chills.

After seven days of fever and body aches, I started to imagine the worst. *I must have a terrible disease. My family will have to go through a second death.*

During that week of flu, in which I imagined some horrific news about my health, I longed for a sense of normal life, of the familiar, of the way life was before Silas died. In that moment, I learned we never long for normal more than when things are abnormal. I was longing for heaven, not just because of the brokenness of earth, but because that brokenness had crashed into my life, taking my son and my health. This longing for things to be made right reminded me that the world was not my home, and that someday, all the broken things will be made right. Until then, this world would not satisfy my deeper longing for complete healing.

After days of putting warm washcloths on my face to ease my pounding head, I began to understand that what I wanted wasn't anything I could find on earth. My son had died. My body ached, walloped by sickness. My world was not right and I could not fix it.

When I finally woke up and my head had stopped throbbing, I realized I had lived through this awful week. The flu did not break me. My son's death would not either.

I needed to fight back against the dark hole into which I was being sucked, to do something that would counteract the physical battle of grief.

I looked at the dog and said, "Do you want to go for a walk?"

Her ears perked up. I pulled out the leash and put on my shoes. I did not want to go for a walk, but I also knew I could not stay inside forever, where the memories threatened to consume me.

Then my friend, Janelle, called one day and asked me if I wanted to walk around the park with her. I told her yes, even though everything inside me begged to stay in the house. I knew that sitting around feeling sorry for myself was not a long-term coping strategy. When I met her in the park, I found that the fresh air and conversation did make me feel somewhat better, if only for the thirty minutes I was outside.

Janelle asked me to walk again the next day, and eventually, we started walking whenever the weather was decent. The more I walked, the more I noticed small things that surprised me: the way the sun reflected off the snow, the change of color in the trees, the soft flow of the river, the way the flowers cascaded over the fencerow. Learning to take care of myself was a lesson in learning to heal.

I knew my heart would be broken for a long time, but that didn't mean that I couldn't see God in my brokenness. When God made his creation and called it good, it was a reflection of his glory. Experiencing his glory each day, even in the midst of my grief, was changing me.

The revelation that gifts could be found in brokenness slowly unfurled in front of me. It didn't fix the death of my son—nothing would do that—but it reminded me I had two choices: the choice to sink into bitterness, anger, and despair or to find God in this mess. The more I did the latter, the more I began to see his gifts slowly emerging in my life. These gifts of brokenness soothed like a healing balm, but it required that I lean into him in my sorrow.

I began to hold on to what lay ahead: a place where the broken are mended, where I would finally understand what this great longing in my heart was all about. It would be a new normal. The long-awaited healing. It would be as things were meant. A heart with no more ache in the deep places. It would be for always.

FIFTEEN

Treasures in the Darkness

T he leaves on the tree were yellow and orange, falling from the sky, soft as snow, leaving a carpet of autumn brilliance on the ground. My dog and I walked through them at the park, hearing the familiar crunching under our feet. All this beauty would soon vanish, one last show before the hard, frozen earth forced the skeletal trees back to stillness and sleep. The rain began slowly, pulling the leaves down to the ground with the drops, covering the paths in a blanket of yellow.

I was learning something through all this pain, as I searched through books, scratched down words, and listened to God-fearing people talk about their suffering. But what I was learning seemed so illogical, so contrary to what we normally believed about suffering: that out of pain, we gained something too, some treasure in the darkness if we were willing to look for it. When we lost something precious, we could find redemption in our pain. Yet, the questions still plagued me in weak moments, when fatigue hit me, when the days fell apart at the seams. *Will I make it through this and find happiness again?*

I wandered through the park, in the midst of colored leaves and dying foliage. The path twisted and turned, past crabapple trees and vivid red maples, past brilliant burning bushes and golden perennials dying in the half-light. I didn't know where I was going. There was no plan, no straight path or clear end to this journey. How much did my own life feel so twisted and turned? Our lives were never straight paths, and yet, if we walked, head down, focused only on the destination, we missed the gift of this journey and the treasures hidden in the dark.

When I was in high school, I wanted to buy a class ring engraved with the school mascot and topped with a colored gem. When I saw the class ring flyer, I fell in love with what was possibly the most expensive and impractical class ring advertised. It was a gold band set with diamond chips. I begged my parents for the ring, but they looked at the price tag and refused.

Instead, my mom offered a solution. "If you really want it, you can get a job and buy your own ring."

They knew of a farm that was hiring corn detasselers, workers who walked up and down the fields and pulled the tassels off the corn by hand in the sweltering midsummer sun. It was a three-week summer job, but it paid well, and I could earn my class ring with only a few weeks of work and still have the rest of my summer free.

I signed up for the job, without really knowing what the work entailed or how physically exhausting it would be. When I showed up for the first day of work, the sun was just beginning to light up the sky as we loaded into an old school bus and were taken to a nearby field, where we were told to pick a row. Up and down the rows I walked, pulling tassels off the corn one at a time, for what seemed like miles of July blue sky. I continued all day until my legs could barely move and my arms hung like weights had been attached to them. At the end of the day, I came home covered in sweat and dirt, with dozens of tiny paper cuts covering my arms and legs from the leaves of the corn stalks cutting my skin.

We worked in every kind of weather, from sweltering heat to thunderstorms that forced us to run for cover so we wouldn't get hit by lightning. After several weeks of back-breaking work, I had enough money to buy the ring. Every time I wore it, I remembered how hard I had worked, and all the sweat and dirt I had endured. This ring was not valuable to me because of the money I spent, but because I had sacrificed something for it. The ring cost me something.

On an unusually cold fall evening, I wore my ring to a high school football game and performed with our marching band for the halftime break. After our performance, we were changing out of our uniforms when I noticed something was missing from my finger. I looked down and realized that my class ring was gone. I had worn it out on the field, but at some point during the show, the ring had slipped off.

I went out to the football field after the game to search for it, walking up and down the lines, from the sidelines to the middle of the playing field, and came up empty-handed. If the ring had fallen off where the game was played, it would have been trampled into the ground and the chances of finding it were slim. I could only think of how hard I had worked and how quickly it was all gone.

I had made a stupid decision to wear my ring on a frigid night and I wanted to go back in time and take it off, so I could keep it forever, or at least until the end of high school. But this was the first of many lessons I needed to face: we don't get second chances to go back and redo our lives.

For a few weeks, I hoped that someone would see my ring, even though I knew it was like searching for a tiny gold fleck in a mountain of sand. As more time passed, my hope of finding the ring faded. Between football games and lawnmowers, the chances of it turning up remained slim. My ring had vanished into a lush green abyss and all my hard work from summer was wasted.

Weeks later, I was performing at a band concert, when the director made an announcement between songs. She shared the story of a student who had lost a class ring at a football game. My face grew hot as I realized she was talking about my unfortunate accident. A band parent who had heard the news had taken his metal detector and swept the field in search of the lost ring.

"Sara, would you come up to get your ring?" the director asked. I sat in shock realizing my band director held the piece of jewelry that slipped from my finger. *My lost ring.*

I walked forward and took the tiny gold circle that had been lost on the football field waiting for someone to find it, just beyond where I could see. Though it was a little dirty and bent, I treasured this gift. I realized when the situation seemed irreparable, that hope was always there. My ring was not gone. I had just lost my way to it.

Only years later, as I sat on my couch missing Silas, would I realize this same principle applied to my own devastating loss. I possessed no way to fix the gaping hole in my life, and no solution to bring my son back, but I could find hope in the darkness. I wanted to make sense of this pain and not waste an opportunity to grow from it. I was searching for the gifts of brokenness—those treasures found only through great loss.

In the midst of my suffering, I realized it was not pain that brought me these gifts, but God. Like hidden treasures, these gifts helped me to understand the greatness of God's love and compassion for me. He was the creator of these gifts, if only I had the eyes to see them. He was the one who could bring light out of darkness and beauty for ashes.

The book of Isaiah says, "I will give you hidden treasures, riches stored in secret places, so that you may know that I am the Lord, the God of Israel, who summons you by name" (Isaiah 45:3).

The English Standard Version of the Bible calls these hidden treasures, "the treasures of darkness." I was learning to find these treasures by going through difficulty and holding on to a fierce hope that God could redeem all the darkness. I looked at the example of a man named Job, who was the poster child for suffering. The Bible says even in the midst of Job's worst nightmare—losing his children, everything he had, even his own health—he still gave thanks, saying, "The Lord gave, and the Lord has taken away; blessed be the name of the Lord" (Job 1:21b ESV).

I wanted to be like Job and bless God no matter the circumstances. I wanted to come out of this stronger and to find that even in my worst pain, God could redeem it. I didn't know if my heart was too broken to find these gifts in the darkness. But I would try to turn these fists into open hands, to open my heart to what might be.

THE FIRST TREASURE

The Gift of Trust

The year after Silas died, I put a basket of fading Easter daffodils in my basement. They were done flowering, the beautiful bloom now dying, but I couldn't bring myself to toss the basket. So instead, I put it on the cold cement floor in our basement, the distant light from a window barely reaching it. It was a hodgepodge of dirt and growth, a symbol of new life—all the things I loved about this season after the cold darkness of winter. But now that the leaves were spindly and thin, I didn't know if the daffodils would flower again. I had to trust that after a season of winter, they would return.

The same was true in this season of brokenness. When I lost Silas, I knew I had two choices. I could let my anger, sadness, and bitterness drive a wedge between me and God, or I could trust that God would carry me through it.

I chose the second option, but it wasn't the easier one. It took way more faith to believe in God when my world came crashing in on me. It would have been simpler to walk away, but instead, I went deep into the messy and hard work of grasping on to faith when life was falling apart. I held on to the belief that God could take my shattered heart and make something beautiful out of it. I clung to hope that no matter how much this hurt my heart, it would not break my faith. God was still good, even in the very darkest places of grief and sorrow.

I wish I could tell you that I knew the path to healing, a Band-Aid that would make the hurt disappear quickly. But healing is a unique journey—there is not one right way, no map to reach the end, no road signs to direct us down the easiest path.

I wanted to find gifts on this journey, not because I think death or brokenness has a silver lining, but because I believe God can do a redemptive work despite the brokenness in my life. In other words,

I believe that in my deepest, most painful moments, God can work in my heart to not only heal, but to make me more like him, and his love won't fail me.

To believe God is good, I had to be able to trust the fact that he would be there for me, that he would not leave me in my time of need, and that he was stronger than any problem I would face. No matter how much my world was shaken, I had to trust he was more powerful than death, and that his love and character would not change in difficult circumstances.

To understand this truth, the Bible gives us examples of God's strength and his protection that shelters us from life's storm. It doesn't mean that his protection will prevent the storms from happening, but that he acts as our refuge when we endure these storms. Psalm 46:1-3 shows us how the Psalmist faced his own personal storm by remembering God's unfailing power.

"God is our refuge and strength,
an ever-present help in trouble.
Therefore we will not fear, though the earth give way
and the mountains fall into the heart of the sea,
though its waters roar and foam
and the mountains quake with their surging."

The Psalmist gives us a picture of a crumbling world—the earth changing in catastrophic ways, while the mountains fall and the waters roar. Yet, even while everything collapses and quakes, God is still stronger. He is our unshakable refuge when everything else falls apart.

When we trust God in our difficult moments, then we're also trusting that he can bring good out of a hopeless situation. When everything falls apart, he does not. In him, not only do we find a shelter to run to during a storm, but a God who can bring unfathomable healing in the midst of it.

In order to trust God fully with our grief, the best thing we can do is read Scripture that confirms who God is and what he did for us on the cross. His sacrifice reveals his unconditional love for us and gives us hope for the future, of living eternally with him in heaven, where all tears will be wiped away and where all pain will be gone. Out of ashes, he gives us beauty. Out of grief comes joy.

When we start to see God as the healer who will pick up the shattered pieces of our hearts and make them whole again, we realize he is our greatest comfort when we are completely destroyed. He will sit with us in our pain and will not leave us when we are at our worst.

We are not left to pick up the broken pieces of our lives. He can take all our brokenness, all our devastating sorrow, and make us whole again. This time, if we allow the pain to draw us closer to him, we will be more beautiful and more complete than before. We will begin to see that he gives us gifts, even in brokenness.

SIXTEEN

Mind the Gap

○—————————————————————————————○

When Silas received his wheelchair at two years old, we pushed him up to the table to join us for dinner since his new wheels were the perfect height. Even though he used a feeding tube for nutrition and didn't eat anything by mouth, dinner was as much a communal event as a dietary one. I hooked his feeding tube to the machine that pumped his formula at the same time we ate our dinner. The decision meant he could no longer experience the pleasure of savoring food and my heart ached every time we ate a pizza piled high with toppings. It was an agonizing choice, but his constant choking forced us to find a less-than-ideal option.

In the world of the sick, we made hard decisions. His ability to swallow had deteriorated to the point he could not even manage his saliva, let alone a piece of meat. If anyone had told me ten years ago I would feed a child through a tube in his stomach, I might have gagged. But learning to do the unthinkable is part of parenthood. We become brave not for ourselves, but for our children, and we are the better for it.

The dinner table was our gathering place, the time in our day when we came together for connection over hot plates of pasta or steaming bowls of soup. It represented all those moments of family life: conversation, the sharing of food, our emotions from the day spilling across our plates. We gathered each night, not just as physical beings, but as emotional and spiritual beings. The habit of sitting down together each night brought meaning to our lives.

But after Silas died, a ragged hole replaced his presence at the table, his blue wheelchair missing from my right side. We all felt the hole we were falling into, that well of grief, the same hole my family struggled with after my father's death.

Twenty-two years earlier, my mother stood at the stove as my sister and I sat down for supper. When she turned around to put the last dish on the table, she stopped and looked at his empty chair. This was our new normal, and his chair was the reminder. My father would never sit at this table again. He would not walk in the door, untie his shoes, and tell us about his day. My sister and I stared at the food, unable to say anything. The awkwardness of silence echoed around the room, before my mom went to her bedroom to mourn this loss in private. No matter how we tried to patch up the grief, there was no way to fix this hole. The empty chair reminded us how our lives had been transformed in an instant.

Now that Silas was gone, our family table had one empty side and it seemed like something had been severed, as if someone had lost an arm. We sat there in gloomy silence until Sam rose, and without saying anything, moved his plate and chair into Silas' spot.

"What are you doing?" I asked.

"I'm going to sit in Silas' place," he said, picking up his glass and then his silverware, and sliding into the space where my son once sat.

That's when I realized what he was doing: he had moved the empty chair. The empty place was no longer where Silas sat, but now where Sam's old seat was. The gap at the table no longer reminded us of what was missing, because now Sam was there. He had filled the empty spot at the table, even if the hole in our hearts could never be filled. We didn't have to be reminded of our grief every time we ate supper.

Early in our marriage, Sam and I went on a trip to England, where we rode the London Underground around the city to see historical sites. The first time we stepped on the train, a recorded voice came over the intercom telling us to "mind the gap." The gap was the space between the train and the edge of the platform, where a traveler could easily trip as they exited the train. They were trying to warn us of a stumbling block, to prevent us from getting hurt, to remember the gap that could cause us to fall.

Now here I was, years later, learning that grief had its own gap to mind, a space between my new life and old, between the before and after. I sensed the gap when I sat at the table and saw the place where Silas sat. I tripped over the gap when I got in my car, and saw an empty seat behind me. When I went into Silas' bedroom and saw his empty bed, the gap seemed wider than ever.

This gap between our old life and new one caused me to stumble on a daily basis and no matter how hard I tried, we could not mind the gap. There would always be something that tripped us up in our grief, to remind us of how life used to be.

Sometimes in our pain, friends and family learn to fill the gap, to change seats, and throw us a life raft so we won't drown. God gives us these people, who in small ways, rescue us from ourselves. They see the empty chair and they fill the gap. From that moment on, my husband sat in Silas' place. This was our new normal. We learned to fill the gap for each other. We learned to extend grace on hard days.

Our neighbors and friends filled the gap too. When Silas died, one neighbor took our dog for the day. Another one babysat our daughter. A third neighbor organized a neighborhood porch lighting in honor of our son. When we pulled onto our street one night, nearly all the porches were lit up. Neighbors we hardly knew had turned on their lights in honor of our son. As we slowly drove down the street, we knew every single light meant that a family was thinking of us. These people were helping us mind the gap of grief the best way they knew how—by remembering our pain.

This need to help one another extends even beyond humans. I once read of an elephant named Eleanor, who was the matriarch of an elephant family in Kenya's Samburu National Reserve. When Eleanor collapsed, the matriarch of another elephant family, named Grace, came to help, and using her trunk, pushed her back to standing. But Eleanor was too weak to stand and fell again, which greatly distressed Grace, who wanted only to help Eleanor to her feet. While her friend suffered, Grace could not leave Eleanor's side.[2] Like those elephants, my friends stepped in to hold me up when I was too weak to help myself.

Tragedy is an inconvenience. But I learned the right kind of friend doesn't see your difficulty as an interruption. Instead, they see it as an opportunity to do whatever needs to be done. People made time and space for our pain, and through that experience, I learned an incredible lesson about prioritizing people's suffering above my own convenience.

Their dedication to serving others revealed my own shortcoming. How often had I seen someone in need and assumed another person would help? Through my worst tragedy, they helped me mind the gap as we stumbled through the darkness.

THE SECOND TREASURE

The Gift of Filling the Gap

After Silas died, our neighbor stopped by and offered to take our laundry. My first instinct was to say no, because laundry feels both highly personal and a little unpleasant. But my mind was on a million other details in the aftermath of Silas' death and the laundry was piling up.

Just say yes, I told myself.

"Thank you," I told her as I handed over my laundry basket, feeling a slight twinge of discomfort. When she returned the clothes later, folded neatly in the basket, I wanted to hug her. *Here is one thing I don't have to remember to do this week.* It was a gift wrapped up in spring fresh laundry scent.

About a month later, friends started calling and texting. "Do you want to get coffee?" "Would you like to do lunch sometime?"

I wanted to say no. The monstrous task of leaving home looking presentable and pretending that I was fine nearly overwhelmed me. Acting like everything was okay, when everything was not okay, meant hard work, more difficult than actually staying home where my feelings, and my old sweatpants, fit me perfectly. But I knew that at some point I needed to face the world, even if that meant putting on real pants.

When I managed to overcome this hurdle of wanting to isolate myself, I realized I didn't die of awkwardness or melt into a puddle of tears. Good friends didn't back down from my pain, no matter how uncomfortable it made them. They sat with me in the suffering. This was a gift in brokenness.

All of us need to find a community of people who are willing to enter into our pain. For some people, the lure of shutting the doors and locking ourselves away is too great. God never designed us for isolation. Our hearts were made for strong connection, healthy attachment, and loving relationships. Our friendships help us heal. They remind us: *You are not alone. I will be there for you no matter what.*

If you're going through disappointment, you were not meant to fill the gap by yourself. God made us for connection and community. Although you don't need crowds of people to walk this journey with you, a few good friends are essential for finding some semblance of normal life. We need friends who do not fear sitting in our darkness until we find the light again.

Over cups of coffee and lunches with friends, I was able to scratch away the surface of my feelings. But at some point, I realized that even good friends couldn't fill the hole of loss completely. There would always be a void, a gap created by the brokenness of this world that was impossible to fill. In that endless ache, I was experiencing the effects of sin and brokenness in our world, a longing to go back to a perfect world. I wanted the Garden of Eden before the Fall, when no death, loss, or suffering existed. I wanted that untainted world back, the place where my son would never suffer from an incurable disease or die. But there was no going back and I could not bridge the gap on my own.

When Adam sinned, we were separated from God and sin poisoned the world. The Fall created a huge gap between us and God with no way to bridge that gap on our own. We have tried to find our way back to God, to fix the brokenness in the world, but because we were sinful, we could not do it ourselves. The gap between us and God could not be bridged through our good works or human decency. It could only be bridged through Jesus. By paying for our sins through his death and resurrection, he was the bridge between us and God, dying so that we could have life eternally. John 5:24 shows us how he filled that gap when Jesus says,

"Very truly I tell you, whoever hears my word and believes him who sent me has eternal life and will not be judged but has crossed over from death to life."

Although I still feel the effects of suffering while I live in this broken world, I know a day is coming when I will see my son again in heaven. The gap has been filled. Because of that hope, I know that someday, I will cup my little boy's face in my hands and never say goodbye again.

SEVENTEEN

Those Who Sit with Us

n high school, I remember going back to school after my father's funeral and everyone treating me like nothing had happened. It was their attempt at making things normal for me. They all knew he had died, but everyone avoided the subject. I found myself caught between wanting life to be normal again and realizing it never could be.

In the months that followed, only two people brought up my father's death. One was my high school English teacher, right before he read a poem about death in front of the class.

"Are you going to be okay with this poem?" he asked me in front of the class. He sat at his desk, book open, ready to read. "Because if you're not going to be okay, you can leave the classroom."

I could feel the class staring at me, trying to figure out if a poem about death would undo me. This invitation read more like an interrogation, and I bristled in my seat, under the weight of this elephant in the room.

"I'm okay," I replied, feeling embarrassment creep up my skin.

Everyone turned to the poem as the teacher began reading, but I could only think about what had happened.

The teacher, trying to be sensitive, had given me permission to leave. But in the moment, it felt anything but sensitive; he implied my grief was an awkward interruption, the thing everyone wanted to avoid talking about.

People wanted me to be okay, but I didn't know how to talk about being okay and I certainly didn't want to talk about it in front of my high school English class. Instead, I wanted someone to ask me how I felt, to sit with me through the ugly stuff, and not ask me to leave. I wanted them to tell me, "It's okay to not be okay." And I wanted them to mean it.

A few months later, I was in the school library reading at a table, when a girl from my class sat down across from me with a book.

We were supposed to be reading, but instead, she asked me quietly, "What is it like to lose a father?"

She waited for my reply and for the first time, I knew she wasn't afraid of the answer.

It's like I had been holding my breath for months, waiting to finally exhale. Someone was brave enough to ask, to bring up the elephant in the room.

I wanted my daughter to have the same kind of friend, someone who accepted her whether she talked or remained silent, a place where people understood that it's *okay to not be okay*. I needed her to know that facing difficulty head-on was better than stuffing the pain. I didn't want her holding her breath, like I had in high school, waiting for someone to ask. Instead, I longed for her to experience a resilient community, people who go through devastating tragedies together, wade through the mess, and come out the other side stronger.

I also knew that she might not find that at school, or with her peers, or even in church. We are not good at bringing up the elephant of grief. We'd rather pretend that life goes on as normal, that healing happens when you pull up your bootstraps and muddle through the pain on your own. Sometimes we try to avoid grief by taking a detour around it, like traffic that's rerouted around a horrendous car wreck. But when tragedy hits, we can't grit our teeth and power through it. We can't avoid the wreckage. There is no easy path to healing. The way to overcome grief involved going right through the middle of it.

That's how I found myself walking up to a storefront in a drab shopping center on a cold November night. The first time we heard about the family grief center, I bristled at the thought of talking to strangers about my pain. I could tell friends, but *strangers*?

The grief center was located in a strip mall where the large storefront windows had been covered with paper. When we walked in, we were ushered down a hall into a brightly lit room where children played board games, while others talked or sat silently. Volunteers arranged pizzas and chocolate milk on a table. I looked around at the sea of faces and realized that all of them were part of this club, a grief group nobody asked to join.

On one wall, hung an art piece made by a child who had participated in the grief center's program. She painted a cheery picture with the words, "Every day it gets a little easier."

When the meal ended, the adults separated from the children for the rest of the evening. We had been given a tour of the children's rooms, walking slowly by the craft room, quiet room, and the hospital room, complete with a patient's bed and medical equipment. Children were invited to role-play doctor and patient scenarios so they could work through their fears of the hospital. But in the volcano room, every kid's favorite stop, children released pent-up anger by beating pillows against padded walls and tearing up phone books.

"Where's our volcano room?" Sam asked, looking at the padded walls. "I need a room like this."

We left Eliana with her group and walked to the adult support group in the room with the covered windows. Some people chatted about their week, while others sat morosely quiet. I sat on an overstuffed couch and hoped no one would ask me any questions.

I'm doing this for my daughter, I told myself. *I don't want to talk to anyone.*

"We'll go ahead and get started," the group leader said. "We always begin our time by introducing ourselves and the loved one who died."

Suddenly a wave of fear pulsated through me that made me want to run from the room. Each person in the circle whipped through their introduction, while I sat dreading my turn. Even though every person there had lost someone, naming my loss scratched open a wound.

When the time came for my introduction, I took a breath and said, "My name is Sara," and then could not get the words out without my voice faltering. "I lost my son, Silas."

Somebody grabbed the tissue box and passed it to me. When I took the box, I looked around and saw that no one looked uncomfortable.

The group leader forged on. "How was everyone's week?"

"I baked a cake for my wife's anniversary," one man said. The anniversary was his wife's death and baking something was a way to celebrate her life. For the first time, it occurred to me that you could remember someone in a way that was not sad.

Someone else shared about her week and how she was struggling to get through her grief. Heads nodded. People cried. The group leader did not offer advice about how to get over loss. She just sat with us in our pain. The group listened without comment and accepted silence as normal. In grief group, *it was okay to not be okay.*

Another week, a new woman sat in our circle and shared that she had lost her husband. She could no longer look at his pictures because it was too painful, so she turned all his pictures around.

When one of her children noticed, they burst out angrily, "Who turned around these pictures?"

Looking down, she told the group, "I couldn't tell him it was me."

For the first time, I began to understand: our losses were different. Our grief was the same. In the months that followed, I learned more about grief sitting on those overstuffed couches than I ever did from reading a book. I thought we were going to grief group for my daughter, but it turned out, I was going to grief group for me.

I had found my tribe, the people who sat with me and did not tell me how to move on, get over it, or find closure. I was starting to understand why the Jews had their own tradition for grief, a process called sitting *shiva* for someone after they lost a loved one. For seven days after a Jewish funeral, the grief-stricken family sits together and mourns. No work is done. The friends who visit during a *shiva call* come in quietly. Tradition suggests the usual small talk is usually replaced by silence or allowing the mourner to open the conversation. Their job is to be present, to sit in the quiet, or listen to the mourners.

In some ways, this group was sitting shiva with me, and in return, I did the same for them. This was our act of survival, a guide for how we would find our way through.

We had lived through overwhelming circumstances and were fighting to save ourselves from the tumultuous current, without letting grief pull us into the undertow. We were swimming for shore, slipping under when we were weak, and then taking a gasp for air and swimming some more. But we were not on this journey alone. We had each other, and that was enough to keep straining for the shore.

One balmy spring evening, the families at the grief center went outside and wrote notes to our loved ones on tiny slips of paper.

"Dear Silas," I wrote, "I miss you so much. I'll see you again in heaven."

I knew my son would never read the note, but writing it somehow made it seem real. We tied the slips to colorful balloons, stood in a circle, and released the balloons together at the same time. In that moment, people were smiling and crying, looking up as the balloons rose higher and higher, our faces pointed toward the sky with hope.

THE THIRD TREASURE

The Gift of Understanding

As we sat in a circle at grief group, one man who was recently widowed, lamented the loss of his wife. "I don't know who to talk to anymore," he said.

The man had friends, but he had lost his best friend, the one with whom he shared everything. In that hole of grief, he found he missed her most in the evenings—when the house was quiet and the world was winding down. It was then that he needed someone to share the mundane details of daily life.

The woman next to him agreed. "I don't have anyone to talk to anymore, either."

For a moment, I realized that in their shared grief, they found something unique—the gift of understanding. It didn't solve their pain, but it did, for a moment, ease the burden of carrying their grief alone.

After I lost my dad, I did not fully understand how to grieve, and stuffed some of my pain without realizing it. When the grief reemerged in my life, I finally faced it with the help of good friends who listened to me cry about my loss and did not offer pat answers in response. They had not experienced the death of a father, but they had an unusual understanding of my pain. I've realized they were the exception, not the rule, when it comes to friendship. My healing took longer than I wanted, but I learned an important lesson: stuffing my grief and trying to move on would not help me heal. I had to give myself time, find friends who would sit shiva with me, and rest in the one who knew suffering and sorrow deeply.

Our culture is not very accepting when it comes to disappointment and loss. At the beginning, everyone sends their sympathies, but as time goes by, people expect that you'll move on from the pain even when you're still deep in the trenches of it. But do we really ever move on?

When few people relate to our pain, we can find comfort in the one who understands the depth of our pain. Jesus was familiar with sorrow. He came to earth with the purpose of suffering and dying so that we could have eternal life with him in heaven.

Isaiah 53:3a says,

> "He was despised and rejected by mankind, a man of suffering, and familiar with pain."

It's easy to buy into the lie that God doesn't understand what we're going through, but the Bible says otherwise. He came to earth to save us and the price he had to pay was with his own life. His suffering became our healing balm.

"But he was pierced for our transgressions, he was crushed for our iniquities; the punishment that brought us peace was on him, and by his wounds we are healed" (Isaiah 53:5).

Jesus gives us the perfect gift of understanding because his life was marked by suffering. He endured the ultimate tragedy and because of this, we can turn to him in our pain.

We also need to find others who understand our complicated feelings. We are not meant to handle difficult journeys alone or carry the load by ourselves. If we can't find these people in our lives now, then reaching beyond our friend circle to find a new group may be necessary. We yearn, for a time, to lean on people who will sit shiva with us. These friends give us the gift of understanding. They do not offer a solution or advice. They learn to sit with us in the pain, and they feel our broken edges, and they do not try to fix us.

The beauty in the gift of understanding is that it's not only one we receive, but one we give back to others. What we learn from friends walking with us through pain becomes a valuable gift that we can share when others face suffering.

EIGHTEEN

The Intersection of Joy and Pain

A few weeks after the funeral, we traveled to Pennsylvania to attend the wedding of my husband's brother and new sister-in-law. I wore a black dress with a scarf, curled my hair, and finally pulled myself together to look presentable, even though inside I was a mess. As a groomsman, Sam spent the day with his family, taking pictures in the rain, posing for a few silly photos in between the serious ones.

I waited with Eliana, but after a while, she found cousins to play with, and I was left alone, standing in an empty sanctuary. I knew people did not expect me to be happy, but I sensed they were not sure what to say, and I did not know how to relieve their awkwardness.

After the wedding, we drove to the reception as rain splattered across the windshield of the van. The sky looked the color of steel wool, mirroring my gloomy mood, but no one at the reception seemed to notice. Weddings represented one of life's great celebrations, alongside the birth of a baby, and these kinds of events counterbalanced life's sad ones.

As I stepped out of my car, a young boy asked me why I had not changed the handicap plate on my van after Silas died. The truth was, I hadn't bothered to, even though I wasn't parking in handicap spaces anymore. I hadn't anticipated the deluge that happened after a funeral—the medical equipment that needed to be returned, the bills that poured in, the piles of documents in my son's name that needed to be changed—these crushing details, on top of grief, buried me. Even worse, I lacked motivation to complete these small, but important tasks. It turns out, grief is a thief, stealing your desire to care about much of anything.

I walked into the reception, where lavish desserts spread across a table and music filled in the silence. People stood around talking, everyone in animated display trying to shout over the music. I found Sam as Eliana disappeared with her cousins again, happy to be free to roam the reception hall. He brought me a cup of coffee and I smiled. He knew how hard it was for me to act like everything was okay. I was limping through the day, pretending to be normal while pasting on a mask over my grief. The ability to feel happiness seemed so far away now, like the distant fading horizon. I was overjoyed for the bride and groom, but I couldn't quite translate that happiness into something tangible for myself.

I didn't understand that when you experience deep disappointment, you often lose the ability to feel joy over the things that used to ignite a spark of happiness. It's not a lasting symptom, but for a time, happiness becomes elusive. The simple pleasures that used to bring joy—going out to eat, spending time with friends—brought no response at all.

During the reception, a man approached us. He was a friend of the family, someone I had met once or twice while in town visiting family.

He smiled and asked us, "How are you doing?"

I looked at my husband, unsure of what to say, since everyone seemed to be avoiding this question. Most people knew we were not fine and they didn't ask. We would have been lying to say otherwise.

"Well," Sam replied slowly, "I just lost my son a month ago." He was trying to soften the blow, although there was really no way to get around it.

The man stammered, "Oh yeah. I meant, how are you doing other than that?"

Other than that. As if there was a part of my life other than that. No part of my life remained untouched by grief. It hung around when I went to bed, when I woke, when I walked in the park, and when I sat at the dinner table. How could I separate it from the rest of my life?

It was not this man's fault that he had forgotten. He hadn't seen us in years. But I didn't know how to explain that grief couldn't be compartmentalized. Instead, it saturated everything, like a filter that colored our whole world.

I stepped away from the conversation and noticed a group of people circling on the dance floor. My daughter was one of them, wedged between some great aunts and a few young cousins. She looked ragged yet wound up, as if she could not dance hard enough. I stood back, a detached observer, watching them move to the music, their faces and bodies animated with the pulsing beat. It was the embodiment of happiness. Then in a few hours it would be an empty hall again, the trash cans full of half-eaten desserts, the tables empty, the lights out. Is this what all of life was, beginnings and endings, and learning to live in the intersection of joy and sorrow?

All eyes watched the dance floor as people bounced and pulsated in a flurry of movement. There was a part of me that wanted to join them, to lean into something other than grief, but I also knew that I could not find what I was looking for on a dance floor. Like a child peering into the window of a home, I watched the party as an outsider.

But I was also starting to realize something else: that I could still grasp joy, even if happiness eluded me. During the wedding ceremony, I found joy in this couple's celebration and the start of their life together. They had each other now, and on their darkest days, when the waves threatened to pull them under, they would hang on to their faith in God together.

I was beginning to understand the difference between the two—joy and happiness—and to realize that just because I had suffered a huge loss, did not mean I lost joy forever. Joy is a kind of enduring emotion, one that buoys us up even when life is bad. Relationships are at the heart of joy, while happiness is based on circumstances, a fleeting moment, a fading emotion. My grief kept me from joining the other dancers that night, but I still found joy in new beginnings, and the hope that in heaven, all would be right again.

Life is made up of beginnings and endings, joy and sorrow, and sometimes the intersection between the two is a strange place to live. But recognizing that all was not lost, that there was still joy to be found in the midst of pain, was a gift that kept me from drowning in my sorrow.

As the music filled the room and dancers swayed and bounced, I pulled my scarf over my bare shoulders, and took the last sip of coffee before going outside, where there was only the black stillness of night.

THE FOURTH TREASURE

The Gift of Joy

Despite my grief, I helped out in Eliana's first-grade class once a week. It became a small sliver of light in my week, the one place I didn't have to think about grief, because I was occupied trying to keep a group of energetic first graders busy. This class was notorious for not listening and talking over the teacher. Children frequently squabbled and kids grew upset over losing a game or being last to take a turn. But they also completely charmed me.

As I arrived, they swarmed like a pack of friendly dogs and peppered me with compliments.

"I like your hair, Ms. Ward," one kid would say.

"I like your shirt," another would add.

Kids wrapped their tiny arms around my waist, like I was some long-lost relative they hadn't hugged in years. It didn't seem to matter that they saw me every week, they were completely surprised every time I walked into class.

While most people tend to shrink from the grief-stricken, these kids were totally oblivious to it. I found relief in being around someone who treated me the same no matter how I was feeling that day. Their joy was found in just *being*.

That day, the teacher asked me to lead a game of Bingo.

"Bingo!" the kids exclaimed with glee as they sat down at the table to grab their game cards. It might as well have been Christmas.

Not long after starting the game, one of the girls stood up and cried, "I got Bingo!" Some of the kids moaned, looking utterly defeated. Apparently, Bingo was a very competitive game in first grade.

"Aw," one boy lamented, "she got Dingo."

"It's Bingo," a few of the kids replied, trying to correct him. But the boy wasn't listening.

"She got Dingo!" he repeated as he pointed at her Bingo card. He was too worried about the fact he had lost the game of "Dingo" to realize he was saying the name wrong. For a moment, his loss had made him oblivious to everything else.

Like this boy, I too easily focused on what I didn't have, rather than recognize the small pleasures that still existed. These kids were teaching me that joy was sometimes found in the places you least expected it, like first-graders' hugs and lost games of Dingo.

They were showing me that joy and pain could reside in the same life at the same time. Like most things, we must intentionally cultivate true, lasting joy, even through difficult circumstances.

We are reminded of this in the Bible when Paul says,

"Rejoice in the Lord always. I will say it again: Rejoice!" (Philippians 4:4)

It's no mistake we're told to rejoice twice. This isn't a command for when life is easy and things are always good. This is a command for all of life, even in the hard times. The key is recognizing that joy is not found in our circumstances, but in our relationship with the Lord.

The word rejoice is the Greek word *chairo*, which means to be glad. It involves rejoicing in many circumstances, which the apostle Paul knew about personally. He wrote the book of Philippians when he was imprisoned and facing trial, knowing that trial would either end in his release or in his death. At that time, he did not know how things would turn out. He told people to rejoice, even while he lived in uncertainty.

Paul's life exemplified joy despite his circumstances. Even though he was shipwrecked, beaten, imprisoned, and almost died, he lived joy—and not just when times were good. He recognized that his inner attitude could be joyful, even when his outer circumstances were not.

I have learned that joy does not depend on my circumstances, but on the one who controls my circumstances. When I can concentrate on Jesus, instead of the chaos and pain around me, it helps me to change my focus to what is joyful in life, even while there is still pain. Worship, prayer, and Bible reading help me lessen the weight of grief and remind me where joy is found, even in the midst of disappointment.

Another way to focus on joy is by remembering how our story ends—that Christ's redemption will make all things right. He will wipe the tears from our eyes. This gives us joy in the waiting, even while we go through hard things.

The other surprise is that our disappointment doesn't have to make us all one layer. We're complex creatures who can feel both the devastation of grief and the elation of joy, sometimes on the same day. Our lives after loss won't be the same, but joy can still be found in unexpected places. We don't have to carry a cross of despair with us forever. This might feel like we're honoring the life we had before, but we're not. Moving toward what this new life looks like, and accepting it as it is, is by far braver.

When we acknowledge that it's okay to feel these dual emotions, we begin to move toward living in the midst of both sorrow and joy. By remembering God's promise of no more tears in heaven, we begin to live fully again (Revelation 21:4). In our pain, we experience joy for the story yet to come.

NINETEEN

Letting Go

His shoe gutted me—a hand-me-down Nike high-top that he had worn the week he died. I found it lying on his bedroom floor, tossed aside carelessly when I was changing his clothes. At more than thirty pounds, and as limp as a sack of potatoes, I couldn't bend down when he was in my arms. So I left the shoe and forgot about it, until I walked into his room.

When I saw that shoe on the floor, the one he had just worn, I broke into tears.

He'll never wear this shoe again.

It lay on the floor casually, like he had kicked it off. The room, still untouched, looked like the room of any small child, pants carelessly tossed into a basket, clothes stuffed into drawers. All these things indicated a life lived and I wanted to stop time and hold it there forever, to pretend like nothing had changed.

Our messes show we are living creatures who exist and create, build and destroy. We don't live in a vacuum where our lives touch nothing. Though my son was not here, his molecules covered every inch of the room. I took the shoe, cradling it in my hands. Then I walked out of the room and closed the door.

Although I knew we could not live with his clothes stacked in his dresser and medical equipment sitting in the room forever, I couldn't bring myself to let go of it either. Giving them up meant letting go of my son and his memories. But the medical equipment in our home took up space, both physically and mentally, and we had no use for it now.

I knew the first step was getting rid of the things that I hated about his disease, all the medical equipment that reminded me that Silas couldn't do basic things like stand, sit, or walk. As much as I associated these things with my son, they served no purpose now. Holding on to them wasn't going to help my healing, nor were they pleasant reminders, so I knew what I needed to do.

But letting go was complicated. These items were intertwined with his identity and my memories of him. He spent all day in his wheelchair. His bed, where he was tucked in every night next to his Woody doll, was the last place I saw him before he died. I feared that if I got rid of all of my son's things, it meant I had to give him up too.

I noticed other people didn't have the answer about letting go either. People who had experienced loss seemed to either get rid of as much as possible or they hoarded too much. It was difficult to find a sensible middle ground when your life has crumbled.

My first task was to get rid of the wheelchair, a bright blue model that looked like a stripped down version of a fancy stroller. I had placed his limp body into that chair dozens of times and had kissed his head as he struggled to hold it up. It had become a part of who he was, and I couldn't seem to separate the chair from him. Now it sat in the corner of our living room, empty.

I found an organization named Wheels for the World that took donated wheelchairs for kids with special needs in other countries. When I arrived at the donation center pushing an empty wheelchair, the secretary pointed toward a vacant spot away from her desk. "You can just push it into the corner," she said.

There was no fanfare, nothing that acknowledged this meant saying goodbye; it was just business as usual. But as I walked out of that place, the significance hit me. I had just given up something special, but that didn't mean I was giving up my son. The severing both pained me and released a newfound freedom. To everyone else, it looked like an ordinary purging session, but to me, this step mattered.

Eventually, I sat down with a large box next to his walnut dresser and opened a drawer. Tiny shirts lay folded in piles. Little pajama sets with *Thomas the Train* on them peeked out from piles of clothes. *Why do these decisions hurt so much?* Silas spent more time in footie pajamas than most kids, and when I lifted up the pajamas and put it close to my face, I could smell the scent of my son, the intoxicating mixture of baby soap and human scent. I read once that smells trigger strong, emotional memories. I discovered this accidentally when I was in the grocery store dairy section and reached into the refrigerator for a gallon of milk. In one deep breath, I smelled my father. He had worked at a creamery and arrived home smelling exactly like the dairy case. For me, it triggered everything I remembered about my father.

So it was no surprise that the smell of my son's footie pajamas elicited the same reaction. It was as if he were there, but painfully, almost agonizingly, he wasn't. I wanted to bottle the scent. I wanted to devour it. I knew realistically that the smell would fade, that boxed pajamas would turn musty over time, but I placed them inside anyway. I could not give them away. Not yet. I went on to the next pair of pajamas and the next, keeping each pair. *Who was I keeping these for?* I already knew the answer. I was keeping them for me. *For me.* A thousand reasons would not change my mind.

It was another part of before and after, of discovering that when one chapter ends and another begins, there was a painful pruning in order to grow again. I had to let go to move on, but I didn't have to let go of everything.

When I finally finished with the clothes, a weary sense of accomplishment settled over me. I was making space, forging a new way in the dark. This emptying of the last chapter of my life was a rite of passage. It would unlock a door where I needed to go, even if I did not want to move forward.

Down the road, I will come across that forgotten box. When I open it, I'll see my son, freshly bathed in his footie pajamas and it will trigger something both painfully hard and exquisitely precious at the same time. It will cut me deep and heal me all at the same time. It will remind me that his story is not over—it's to be continued on the other side.

THE FIFTH TREASURE

The Gift of Hope

One day, while dinner roasted in the oven, I began sorting through a shelf in a closet, finding a whole pile of paperwork with Silas' name on it. I glanced through the stack, finding prescription drug instructions, a calendar charting seizure activity, and his speech therapist's looping handwriting. I held the papers in my hand, unsure what to do with them.

These papers were some of the few links to Silas' last years, a reminder that he lived, his existence validated in writing. Though not pleasurable memories, in an odd way, I found their familiarity comforting. Now he no longer needed a doctor or physical therapy. He didn't need injections, medications, or surgery. These medical documents were reminders of his brokenness, but God's promises reminded me that he was healed. This was choosing light over the darkness, hope over despair. In Psalm 42:5, the Psalmist asks,

Why, my soul, are you downcast?
Why so disturbed within me?
Put your hope in God,
for I will yet praise him,
my Savior and my God.

The word hope in this Psalm is the Hebrew word *yachal* and it means to wait on God. It describes a dependency on him, trusting what he says is true even when our feelings say otherwise. This Psalm reminds us that God makes good on his promises. When we feel abandoned and alone, we have to remember that despair is not the end of our story. We put our hope in God's promise to redeem this world and all the brokenness in it.

It also reminds us that our hope is not dependent on our circumstances or what we can see around us. It is easy to fall into despair when life is hard and start to believe the lies we tell ourselves:

Nothing good will ever happen to me. God must not love me or else it would have worked out. Why doesn't God hear my prayers and answer me?

Waiting is not a sign that God has forgotten. It's not a measure of his love. It doesn't mean he has not heard you. Hope means waiting on God and trusting in what we know is true. This means remembering to focus on the unseen rather than the seen.

Paul reminds us of how we can change our focus in 2 Corinthians 4:16-18 when he says,

"So we do not lose heart. Though our outer self is wasting away, our inner self is being renewed day by day. For this light momentary affliction is preparing for us an eternal weight of glory beyond all comparison, as we look not to the things that are seen but to the things that are unseen. For the things that are seen are transient, but the things that are unseen are eternal." (ESV)

In this section, Paul uses contrasting words to compare this life to the one in heaven. It's a lesson in opposites to help us catch a glimpse of the glory of heaven compared with the frustrations of earth.

First, he tells us that our afflictions are light and momentary. We often describe our troubles by saying they weigh heavy on us. Grief, suffering, and loss bring a burden to our lives and make us believe they will last forever. But Paul wants us to have an eternal perspective, to look at our troubles as only light and temporary compared to the eternal weight of glory mentioned in the Bible. He uses the word weight to describe the incredible glory we'll experience in heaven. This kind of weight isn't a burden like our troubles are, but gives us hope that we will experience an indescribable new life, one without pain or sorrow. In heaven, our burdens will pass away and there will only be joy forever.

He also tells us not to fix our eyes on what is seen, which includes our circumstances and the world around us, but on what is unseen—being in heaven with Jesus. He reminds us, in closing, that this world is transient, it will pass away, but heaven will be forever. By changing our focus from our present circumstances to eternity, it allows us to cling to hope even when our days are grim.

Hope changes the way we see our lives. It turns our world upside down and shakes out the pockets of all those things we depend on, like ambition and worldly success. It forces us to put our trust in something we cannot see. Hope shows us that the temporary pain of life is a vapor, but what matters is keeping our focus on Jesus, who never fails us.

TWENTY

Small Victories

○—————————————————————————————————○

I was pushing my grocery cart through the meat section of the grocery store, when I began to feel a growing sense of panic. I hadn't anticipated fear and worry showing up right there in the middle of the ground chuck. My heart began to beat wildly as I tried to get myself under control. I stopped my cart, worried that I was having a heart attack, and pretended to look at the cuts of meat as people wandered by, oblivious to the screaming siren that was going off in my head. I suddenly wanted to abandon my cart and flee the store just so I wouldn't collapse in the middle of the rump roasts. Then it hit me: *I am not dying. I am having a panic attack and my fight-or-flight instinct is telling me to run.*

I knew about some of the side effects of grief: uncontrollable crying, depression, insomnia, sleeping too much, and a lack of joy. But I hadn't expected the twins of fear and worry to show up. I had mistakenly believed that my fears ended after Silas died, since I no longer had to worry about him passing away. But what I had forgotten was that after a traumatic event, when I least expected it, fear and worry would come barreling out of the dark.

This was not my first panic attack. After Sam had cancer, I had several panic attacks, but had no idea what they were or why I was having them. The first one happened when I was speaking at our Mothers of Preschoolers group, when I had been asked to share about my husband's cancer journey. In the middle of speaking, my heart began to beat erratically, like it was a Mexican jumping bean exploding in my chest.

Public speaking is a major fear for many people, but that wasn't usually a problem for me. Talking about my husband's cancer journey forced me to relive the details of his ordeal and my body reacted with a pulsating fear that ran through me like a Mack truck. I realized that all of what we went through—the surprise diagnosis, multiple surgeries, the horrendous chemotherapy—was now playing itself out in my body physically. Recounting his story was the trigger that caused me to panic. Until then, I had suppressed these feelings of fear by convincing myself that I was fine, but I was *not* fine. My body needed a way to process my fear and did so in the only way it knew how: by freaking out.

Our brains are hardwired with a fight-or-flight response. This is the same response that tells us to run from our enemies or fight when danger shows up. The only problem is, after trauma, our brains start to become triggered by things that aren't actually dangerous. We suddenly start anticipating all kinds of horrible things that could happen and our bodies respond with panic.

When I was struggling through this, I craved God's peace in my life to overcome my fear. I wanted to be healed so that these panic attacks would subside. Unfortunately, the world tells us some very misleading things about finding peace. Namely, that we can make peace with what happens on our own and that it is attainable if we can come to terms with our past. Well-intentioned people push us to stop wrestling with the question of why this happened and move on to acceptance. But problematically, we can't stop wrestling with the question until we understand *the why* behind our wrestling.

The reason we can't find perfect peace on our own is because God didn't design our world to be a place of suffering. The Garden of Eden was perfect until the fall of Adam, but now creation groans under the weight of sin, brokenness, and death (Romans 8:22). This is why I lament the loss of perfection. I want Eden back and I crave the peace that an orderly and perfect world would bring. My son's death and my husband's cancer aren't things I can come to terms with because these devastating events were not part of the original Eden. During my panic attack, my body was crying out because my life was anything but peaceful and I couldn't fix it.

When I accepted the reality that only God could provide peace, I also accepted that fear was part of my world. I couldn't fix myself. I could only recognize my panic for what it was. Part of our fallen world. When another one hit, I forced myself to lean into the fear and call it out for what it was.

It's just a panic attack, I told myself.

And remarkably, it worked. Like a child who's shown there are no monsters under the bed, I needed the reminder that I was not dying a sudden death. The panic didn't disappear, but it slowly receded, like a pounding wave that pulls back from the shore.

Silas' death brought on the second wave of panic attacks, but this time I knew how to deal with my post-traumatic stress: I breathed deeply and told myself I was not dying. I faced the panic by naming my fear and letting myself experience it, even if that meant feeling vulnerable in the middle of the grocery store.

In her popular book, *Daring Greatly*, Brené Brown defined vulnerability as "uncertainty, risk, and emotional exposure."[3] Although Brown touts vulnerability as a strength, for a fearful person, embracing uncertainty and risk would be like hugging an archenemy. When someone told me there would be days I'd feel crazy during my grief, they never told me it involved having panic attacks in odd locations. That's because none of us knows when our fear buttons will get pushed. For me, it was the grocery store, but for someone else, it might be a back-to-school night with the kids. Either way, I had to learn to lean into the uncertainty and accept my vulnerability to dispel my anxiety. In order to move forward from my loss, I had to move forward from my fear. They were intertwined and inseparable.

With a pounding heart, I headed to the grocery store and slowly walked up and down the aisles. As I approached the dreaded meat section (which was now forever associated in my brain as Panic Attack Central), I took a deep breath and pushed the cart to the place where fear had gripped me like a vise. I was willing to feel vulnerable, to face fear head-on. This time, no fear rose up and threatened to topple me.

Instead, my heart beat steady. I breathed deep. Today, this was my small victory.

THE SIXTH TREASURE

The Gift of Vulnerability

I grew up in a culture where I was taught to "pull myself up by my bootstraps" and "make do" when things went wrong. It was a very Midwestern, German-American mindset. But somewhere along the way, this overemphasis on grit became an obstacle for me. After going through some major losses, I couldn't pull myself up by my bootstraps. I no longer could overcome my fears on my own. Recognizing that I needed help was the first step toward healing, and a mindset that focused more on God-dependency than self-sufficiency.

When I was a very little girl, one of my earliest memories was a dream where I was standing at the top of a steep staircase in my house. As a small child, I could not get down the stairs on my own and if I attempted to try, I would most likely tumble down the steps. In my dream, an angel appeared; he took my hand and led me down the steps. As a child, feeling vulnerable and then asking for help was natural. But somewhere along the way, I had bought into the idea that I needed to be strong and wise, and that vulnerability was weakness.

But that's not what the Bible says about weakness. In 1 Corinthians, weakness is seen as strength.

"Brothers and sisters, think of what you were when you were called. Not many of you were wise by human standards; not many were influential; not many were of noble birth. But God chose the foolish things of the world to shame the wise; God chose the weak things of the world to shame the strong."
(1 Corinthians 1:26-27)

The first step in recognizing vulnerability as a gift is understanding that God accomplishes his purposes through our weaknesses. He uses the fragile and foolish things of this world in order to show his sovereignty and glory, otherwise we would be tempted to take the glory from God. We would try to boast in our cleverness and strength, instead of recognizing that he alone deserves the honor.

When we try to lean on our worldly accomplishments, like our careers, successes, and achievements, then we are less likely to see our flaws and sinful tendencies. By recognizing our weaknesses, we are not tempted to put on a facade of self-sufficiency.

Vulnerability also teaches us that we can't get through life without a community of friends. When Silas died, we couldn't manage our overwhelming grief by relying on our human wisdom and problem-solving natures. Recognizing this weakness was the only way to open myself up for receiving help. People came alongside us to fill the gap and remind us that God had not forgotten our needs when we were in the valley of despair. Friends bought groceries and babysat, while others sat with us in our grief and just listened. People prayed for us when we were too weak to pray for ourselves. Our friends took their turns helping, and reminded us of who God was and that he would not leave us. He provided help so we would not be alone in our pain.

Our heartbreak was a slow laborious journey with no set ending, but God was reminding me that he would carry us through this heartache. I no longer had to pull myself up by my bootstraps. Instead, Jesus met me in my weakness and showed me I could depend on a sovereign God who held my future in his hands. This didn't mean it was a simple or quick fix. But if we're willing to lean into our pain and trust in a sovereign God—to be vulnerable with him—then in our weakness we find his strength.

TWENTY-ONE

Kicked Out of the Club

When my son's health was at his worst, we learned to keep our lives small, to not travel far, in case we had a medical emergency. Though I missed traveling, it seemed far easier than trying to travel with a medically fragile son. We hunkered down and stayed home, but when Silas died, a door to the world suddenly opened. No longer were we strapped to home. No longer did I have to say no to traveling more than three hours away.

"Hey, there's a spot open on this church trip," Sam told me one day. "You could still go if you wanted to."

Even though I wasn't exactly feeling like a social butterfly, the thought of Florida sunshine in January sounded good and I thought that volunteering might take my mind off things in the meantime. We would be working at a nonprofit organization called Give Kids the World that provided weeklong, cost-free vacations to children with life-threatening illnesses and their families. These families, who are typically visiting Disney World, received free accommodations through the Make-a-Wish Foundation and got to enjoy all the amenities of the resort. Serving kids with life-threatening diseases in a happy place seemed like a good idea even if my heart was a little wrung out from grief.

Only three months had passed since Silas had died, and our plans to go on a Make-a-Wish trip to Florida and stay in this same location had been cut short. On the one hand, I looked forward to getting away and doing something other than feeling gloomy. On the other hand, I was worried that all I would do was think about Silas.

A few months later, Sam and I packed our bags for Florida and went to work in the cafeteria, where we filled cups with soda, carried trays of food for families, and wiped off tables. The cafeteria resembled a cheerfully decorated restaurant filled with stuffed animals, candy stripes, and storybook characters. As I was carrying trays, I noticed a family who had two kids who were in wheelchairs. One of the children was fed by a G-tube, while the other could only eat by mouth as long as the parent fed him. While sitting at the table, the dad carefully poured formula into his child's feeding tube. He patiently sat there waiting, holding the syringe that slowly drained the milk down the tube into his daughter's stomach, while the families at tables around him shoveled eggs, sausage, and toast into their mouths.

It reminded me of all the times I delayed eating to prepare Silas' feeding tube. I wanted to say something to the man, to let him know I understood what it was like to be in his shoes, but I hesitated. We had been told not to ask questions about the kids and their medical conditions. This was their family vacation, a chance to escape from all of the daily burdens of living with a disease, without dealing with curious onlookers.

I snuck glances at them as I brought families refills on their drinks. After they fed their children in the wheelchairs, they finally began eating, then packed up their medical supplies and wheeled their kids out the door.

Another man entered the cafeteria with his child, carrying a familiar looking bag of formula and G-tube supplies. The cafeteria wasn't as busy, with empty tables spread out across the room. I walked up to him and said, "Your G-tube supplies remind me of feeding my son."

The man looked startled and didn't say anything. I realized the mistake I had made bringing up the topic of feeding tubes without warning. What was I thinking? I hadn't even introduced myself. I smiled awkwardly and walked away, realizing I had said too much.

That's when it hit me. *I'm not one of them anymore.* I was excluded from the club of parents who had children with life-threatening illnesses. My child was no longer fed with a feeding tube or used a wheelchair. If I tried to explain to them that I understood, they would only hear my sad ending and hope theirs wasn't the same.

Standing in the restaurant with a dripping washrag, I realized that not being in the club should be a relief, but it felt like loss. I wanted my son with me, to be one of the families carrying bags of medical supplies and formula around an overcrowded, humidity-drenched Disney park. Nobody had warned me how angry I would feel about being kicked out of the club—the same club I had begged not to be a part of in the first place.

Now I was in this strange place, stuck between the world I used to know and the new place into which I was thrust without warning. I knew I wasn't alone in being kicked out of the club—this happened to those who move from the married club to the singles club, or when your child is diagnosed with a serious disease and you are forced into the sick child club. It doesn't matter how much you rail against being kicked out of the club. The world now sees you differently. Your identity has shifted, whether you like it or not.

After working at the cafeteria for several hours, Sam and I drove a special tram around the resort complex. Most families were still at the parks this evening, so we circled a vacant vehicle around an empty resort, until Sam asked, "You want to drive it?"

I had never driven a tractor, let alone a tractor designed to shuttle families, but since the park was mostly empty, it seemed like a good time to learn.

"Okay," I said, crawling into the driver's seat. Since there was an extra pedal on the floor and I had no idea how to use it, I got my first lesson in driving a tractor with a manual transmission. Several attempts later, I was steering the tractor around the park with no more rocky starts.

As we listened to the engine's hum and circled the deserted resort, I thought about what it would have been like to stay here with Silas. I tried to imagine tucking him in bed in one of the storybook villas or taking him for a ride in the tractor I was driving. I imagined us eating in the cafeteria as a family, our plates piled high with pancakes.

I grappled with holding up two versions of my life: what might have been and what was. We circled the park, a slow train moving in the dark, as I watched my old life fade. I would never stay here with my son. I would not sit at a table in the cafeteria, or go on the carousel, or ride the tram with Silas. I would let go of those dreams, like a distant train moving across the landscape.

I was learning to let go, but I was learning to be found too. I was discovering that no matter how much I changed because of the brokenness, some things did not. God was still the same. No matter what else changed in my life, my identity in Christ had not. I would always be a child of God, no matter what I lost or let go of. He would meet me even in the hard and messy places. He would reveal the beauty found in the brokenness. He would show me this wasn't the end of my story, even as I watched the slow train of what might have been disappear into the dark.

THE SEVENTH TREASURE

The Gift of Identity

Walk into any nursery or daycare center and you'll see the same scene played out every day. One child has a prized toy they don't want to give up and they protest vehemently when they are forced to let go, screaming, "It's mine!"

I know this pain too. When things have been taken away from me, I have railed against how unfair it seemed, justifying my anger by explaining how I deserved it. Other times, I've cried in despair, while wallowing in the darkness of self-pity.

For a long time, my first identity was as a wife and mom. But when you lose somebody, the world sees you differently. A widowed woman I know was excluded by some of her married friends, because she no longer fit into the married club. She didn't want to be kicked out of the club and her feelings were crushed at being left out. Our world has this strange way of ripping off labels when life changes and most of the time, we are not even aware of how much it hurts.

One of the most painful identities to lose was being Silas' mom. Even though I will always be his mother, I realized on the trip to Florida that I had to go back to the core of who I was and claim my God-given name as a child of God. I have learned, rather painfully, that all the things I think are mine can be taken in a moment. Being called mom or wife is a true gift, but these gifts are not ours to control and learning that lesson was one of the most painful ones.

Even though our identities might change over time, God never leaves us without an identity in him. No matter what we go through, no matter how many times our identity shifts, his does not. In the uncertainty, I still knew one thing was true: I am his. When the world is turned upside down, this is the one thing we can hold on to. No matter what else is taken from me, my identity in him can never be taken away.

The Bible reinforces this identity as God's children in 1 John 3:1a,

> "See what great love the Father has lavished on us, that we should be called children of God! And that is what we are!"

The Father's love for us is so incredible that he invites us to be part of his family. When we believe in him, we become his sons and daughters—an identity we are given for eternity. "Yet to all who did receive him, to those who believed in his name, he gave the right to become children of God" (John 1:12).

As we let go of what we thought was ours, we learn to lean harder on the promises God gives us for eternity. Like Jacob wrestling the angel (Genesis 32:22-31), we might wrestle with the loss of our old identity, but what we are given in return—an identity in him that can never be taken away—is a gift that heals us from the deepest of wounds.

When life unravels, it isn't my old identity that vanishes. I was, and still am, Silas' mother. But I have a new identity that can never be stripped from me. No matter what changes in the world's eyes, I am always a child of God. That is something that can never be stolen. Not by loss. Not by brokenness. Not by death. My whole world can crumble, but none of this alters the fact that I am loved by God. In every place, I am his.

TWENTY-TWO

Love Heals

D uring Silas' many hospital stays, Sam and I found every restaurant we liked within walking distance. We ate from bags of takeout food next to our son's bed and drank sodas from the hospital refrigerator down the hall. I downed horrible cups of coffee from the hot drink machine and occasionally splurged on lattes from the hospital café downstairs. This was the closest we came to a date.

Practical reasons kept us from going out to eat with our son when we were home. Since he couldn't swallow food, it seemed unfair to drag him to a place that smelled like the one thing he couldn't have. So we avoided restaurants, except when we were in the hospital, because this meant we ate either in a mediocre cafeteria or grabbed takeout from a restaurant.

"What do you want to eat?" Sam asked as I sat next to Silas' hospital bed.

"That Thai Soup," I'd say. "Extra spicy."

A bag of takeout in a hospital room was a sorry excuse for a weekend night, but it was the best we could do. We slurped soup and flipped TV channels as the IV pumped fluid into my son's arm.

While our life was on hold, friends' lives continued without us. They threw parties, hosted baby showers, and gathered for barbecue dinners while we sat in a hospital room eating lukewarm noodles from a takeout box.

This survival technique, paring life down to just us, left our relationships neglected like a wilted houseplant. Friendships suffered, my phone stopped ringing, playdate invitations evaporated. Like squeezing the juice out of a lemon, it squeezed out all the time left for anyone else.

Our whole life focused on keeping Silas alive. Everything else slowly shriveled from lack of attention. Our marriage was no exception. How do you go on a date night when you've been sleeping on a hospital couch? Later, I saw all the areas in my life that were limping along due to neglect—namely, my health, my marriage, and friendships.

To remedy the situation, we began visiting restaurants all over the city: the hole-in-the-wall Thai place with the spicy panang chicken curry, the Mexican restaurant with the chorizo tacos and Spanish commercials blaring from the TV, and the neighborhood soup-and-sandwich joint that left our clothes soaked in greasy smoke.

In conversations over crab rangoon and Vietnamese beef pho, we discovered that even though we loved our son well through his life, his disease consumed every moment. His survival became our united goal. Over bowls of fragrantly spiced tikka masala and steaming red pepper-gruyere soup, we finally talked about all the things we could not say before. Together we could survive this. We carried the pain as one. We let grief unite us.

When we acknowledged the neglect that happened over years of hospital visits, we knew what we needed to do. Start over. Rebuild the connection. Find in the rubble of our lives something beautiful again.

After our week working at Give Kids the World, we had one free day to do whatever we wanted. It had been six years since we had taken a trip with no kids and we were not about to let grief ruin our fun. We opted to go to Universal Studios, where they had recently opened a section called The Wizarding World of Harry Potter.

Both of us consumed the ubiquitous wizarding series when they came out, preordering the books so they arrived on our doorstep the day they were published. It was not surprising then that the wizarding world was the one destination we would choose to go, a place that had no connection to our son. It reminded us of those glorious pre-children days when we could escape into a book without interruption on a Sunday afternoon.

When we arrived, we entered Hogsmeade, a quaint, cobblestone street with its bewitched window scenes and snow-covered rooftops. We hardly noticed the crush of the crowds as we waited in line at Hogwarts or stopped for a magic wand demonstration. We meandered through the magical scene, guzzling foamy butter beers and marveling at how strange it felt to be here without any children who needed us to tie their shoes or take them to the bathroom. We tried on costume pieces and took selfies in silly hats, giggling in the back of Honeydukes.

I didn't think about Silas until we walked through a Dr. Seuss-inspired section and sadness fell over me as I saw parents with young children enjoying the colorful rides. We were having so much fun exploring the ornate details of Hogwarts and marveling over the picturesque village of cottages and shops that neither one of us had even mentioned his name. It was the first time I had forgotten my grief in months, and the realization brought up both sadness and guilt. *How can I have so much fun without my son?*

"Do you want to ride the Hulk roller coaster?" Sam asked. "It's just on the other side of this section."

"Sure," I said. No young children would ride the Hulk because they wouldn't be tall enough to make the height cut. For a few minutes, I could forget about my feelings while being yanked and spun upside down a thousand times.

As we got in line for the coaster, I suddenly became aware that we were some of the oldest people there. Even though we were only in our thirties—certainly not old in my book—the line was filled with mostly teenagers, a sure warning sign that I should have skipped the ride. As we went up the first hill, I heard the slow *click, click, click* of the coaster before it dropped into a free fall. My stomach did the same, while my head bounced against the headrest like a rubber ball.

Not having ridden a roller coaster for almost a decade, I had forgotten how thrill rides were intentionally designed to throw you around like a punching bag. We spun and twirled and careened upside down, while my head was pummeled in every direction.

When the ride finally came to a stop, I noticed my neck was stiff and tender, while Sam held his stomach, his face drained of color. We were hoping to feel like kids again, but instead, we felt sick.

"I think I need to sit down," Sam said, looking pale.

"Why don't we get something to drink?" I suggested.

We wandered over to the nearest hamburger joint, ordered sodas, and sat outside in the sunshine. I rubbed my neck as Sam downed his drink. Despite the sensation that I had been kicked in the head, the sunshine settled me.

"I guess we're not as young as we used to be," he said, managing to smile.

"We're like a couple of old people, between my neck and your stomach," I said rubbing my shoulder.

We both started laughing. Even with our aches and pains, I recognized what a gift it was to laugh with someone who had walked with me through my darkest hour, someone who had seen me in ripped sweatpants and tangled hair and loved me anyway. Sometimes, the closest thing to love was hanging on when life felt like a free fall.

Together we grasped the glorious hope of how much more laughter must be on the other side, when all things would be made new in heaven. We had been through a lifetime of searing grief together and had discovered along the way, if we let the pain forge us as one and not tear us apart, we could make it through.

In the end, we were left picking through the ashes and remaking our lives from the rubble. That was where the hard work of love began—in the rebuilding, when we realized we had nothing left. That was when I rediscovered all the reasons I fell in love in the first place. Sometimes I found it in the strangest places, like in the middle of a theme park, and other times, over a box of pad Thai.

This time, all I had to offer was my brokenness and the willingness to try again. Somehow, trying again was enough to rebuild what was never completely lost, but only needed to be found again. It began over a takeout soda and the discovery that all the reasons why we fell in love were still there after all.

THE EIGHTH TREASURE

The Gift of Love

As a little girl I loved the story of Cinderella, not just because she transforms into a princess, but because the story always reaffirmed my belief that love conquers all. Whenever I doubted this, I just watched a Disney movie to prove that love won over everything—the disapproving parents, the smarmy women, the evil bad guys.

In some ways, love has become the hero of our story and I want to be rescued just as desperately as everyone else. For example, on a regular basis I am lucky enough to stumble across huge centipedes in my house. I hate centipedes, bottom-of-my-heart despise them, and they seem to know this and surprise me by waiting behind closed doors. When I walk into the bathroom and see one sitting benignly in the shower, instead of smashing it with my shoe, I run away and find my husband to do the dirty work for me. Let's face it: there is nothing that says love more than Sam killing the bugs I don't like—spiders, centipedes, and a few rogue beetles. Every time he kills one, I fall in love with him all over again. Yes, love does conquer all, even centipedes in the bathroom.

Whatever your love-conquers-all moment is, we continue to buy into this belief that love won't fail us, and we want to believe it so badly. But surprisingly, love falls apart under continual pressure. It can be broken with betrayal, wither in neglect, and be crushed under grief. Love, it turns out, is as vulnerable as we are.

I wish I didn't feel so frustrated every time my husband forgets to say "I'm sorry" or take out the trash. But he does, and I do the same. I disappoint him regularly. I frustrate him often. I'm all the things that love is not.

So if love conquers all, then why do I seem to be failing at it so badly?

We often think of love as formidable, strong, and capable of withstanding all attacks, but our relationships are not immune to the battering of life. Relationships, in their best moments, feel like fortresses, but really, they are more like sandcastles on a beach. They can't withstand the tide on their own, but instead, must be constantly tended and rebuilt. When the tide is out, the sandcastle remains much like how it was constructed, like our relationships during the good times of life. But when the tide comes in, little parts of the castle start to sink. Every time pounding waves wash portions away, it has to be remade, and more sand is gathered to replace what gets washed away.

Like sandcastles, loving relationships do not stay close on their own. As people and circumstances change, so does our need to love people as they change too. This means building our bond even when life tears it down. Love can heal us, but it takes work to build it back up again. It takes trying again, even when you have nothing to give.

It would have been all too easy for us to fall into the trap of believing that because we lived together, we would connect with each other throughout the week. But without intentional moments of connection, we would not take the time to love each other well.

Even with these intentional habits, we were broken people who could only love each other in imperfect ways. We both recognized there was only one perfect love who could help us through our brokenness. God's love doesn't falter when the pounding waves crash into it. He is the fortress we can run to when we're being battered by life. Psalm 144:2 reminds us,

> "He is my loving God and my fortress,
> my stronghold and my deliverer,
> my shield in whom I take refuge."

The only perfect love is God's love, because he is the only perfect one who can give us a love that never fails. At our lowest point, his love can be a shelter through any storm. When our lives unravel, he will never let us down. The world might fail us. Our friends may abandon us. But God's love heals us.

———————————————

TWENTY-THREE

The Mountains Bear the Scars

For months, I wanted to wake up and not feel the weight of loss. I wanted to open my eyes and see something new, a place with no strings attached to the life I had before, no painful memories to sort through. Something in me wanted to spring up, like a green shoot fighting through the dead earth of winter.

We decided to go west and settled on the Rocky Mountains, where we rented a small cabin in Estes Park. We made the trek, all eighteen hours of it, in two days, holed up in a van packed to the top of the seats. When we stopped at a rest stop, a field of sunflowers grew in the ditch alongside weeds. They were proof that lovely things could grow in harsh places, where dust was stirred up from trucks bearing down at eighty miles per hour. At the edges of untended fields, where fences met no man's land and weeds choked everything else out, the sunflowers managed to thrive. They made beautiful the untamed fencerows where I least expected to see beauty. If God could make these sunflowers grow in the wasteland of road edges, perhaps he could cultivate something extraordinary in my life too.

When we finally crossed into Colorado, a rocky landscape began to swell up before us. Mountains appeared in the distance and grew bigger with each mile, until they swallowed us and we lost the distant horizon. These mountains would become our hideaway, an escape where we could marvel at the snowcapped mountains. No wonder the Psalmist wrote:

I lift up my eyes to the mountains—
where does my help come from?
My help comes from the Lord,
the Maker of heaven and earth. (Psalm 121:1-2)

Chapter 23

If God designed these mountains to withstand thousands of years of storms and cold, then surely he could help me make it through my own troubles.

Upon arrival, we signed up for a horseback ride in the mountains. The trails took us through open fields filled with wildflowers and along narrow paths next to steep cliffs. The horses pushed on, their hooves striking rock and gravel that became the soundtrack for our ride. As we climbed the mountainside, the horses kept their heads down, looking for a good foothold. On a narrow section next to a steep drop-off, my horse stumbled on a rock. In that moment, I felt his strong, confident stride weaken as he fought to regain his footing. This muscular animal, who knew the trail as well as any guide, was still as vulnerable as the rest of us. One ill-placed step could become his downfall. I gripped the reigns tighter and avoided looking down the steep drop.

Later, a horse in front of me stumbled hard and fell to the ground, rolling to his left side. The startled rider scrambled away before the horse rolled on her leg. The trail guides galloped over to help, but not before the horse jumped back to his feet. The girl stood, surveying the powerful horse that almost crushed her leg.

"Do you want to get back on the horse?" the trail guide asked her after a few minutes. Pale and shaken, she nodded and stepped into the stirrup.

Despite the rugged beauty of chiseled rocks, the mountains possessed an ugly side. Sometimes, we came across scorched patches of land. Charred trees lay on the ashy ground, a wasteland where no life existed. Everything that had grown in this area was now dead, burned to dust by the park, which used prescribed fires to control the unnatural buildup of dead and diseased trees. Although I only saw the scarred remnants, the rangers knew this process would result in a rebirth of the land. This was part of the life cycle of a forest, even if it only looked like a seared wasteland. It was hard to imagine that from these ugly scars, life could break through.

In our culture, we see scars as imperfections, like a visible reminder of pain. My husband bears a scar that runs from his sternum to pelvis, splitting his body into two parallel halves. The scar resulted from two separate surgeries, one he had as a baby and cancer surgery as an adult. As an infant, he suffered from severe projectile vomiting, and was diagnosed with pyloric stenosis, a condition when the muscle between the stomach and intestine swells and blocks food from entering the intestine. For an infant, the lack of nourishment becomes life-threatening, but once a baby had surgery, there were no long-term side effects. Afterward, the only reminder was a scar across a baby's perfect, tiny belly.

Almost thirty years later, Sam's oncologist used the same scar from his pyloric stenosis surgery, but extended it further across his body. His scar became a symbol of surviving not just one, but two life-threatening conditions. It represented life and healing, a reminder of God's mercy through every circumstance.

Our scars shape us in ways we could never have been changed otherwise. They tell a story of struggle and pain, and how in the end, God brought us through. He redeemed our brokenness, and out of the pain of our lives, something new was born. The mountains bear the scars and so do we.

As I watched Eliana and Sam on their horses in front of me, I knew that we would make it through this grief together. We would get back on our horses and face our fears. We would look at our scars and not see something ugly, but beautiful. We'd see it as proof that in our healing, we chose to be brave.

THE NINTH TREASURE

The Gift of Healing

Sam was at a pool one summer when a kid pointed to the scar on his abdomen and asked, "What is that?"

"It's a scar from surgery," he replied. Most of the time, kids stare at his scar with an equal mixture of curiosity and repulsion.

In a world where scars are considered imperfections, we've forgotten that we need scars in order to heal, because without them, we'd be walking around with gaping wounds. When our skin becomes injured, the body produces collagen fibers to repair the damage. These collagen fibers produce a different texture in the tissue than in the skin around it, but the process is a necessary part of the skin's healing. The scar demonstrates, not imperfection, but healing, showing that even though we went through something hard, we are changed by it.

Just as a physical scar is part of the natural healing process, so our internal scars are part of our emotional healing process. They bring a depth and complexity to our lives, which help us to understand other people's pain. We're no longer perfect people with perfect lives. Instead, we're bruised and broken, and with that comes a wisdom forged only through the fire of trials.

If we want to become more like Christ, then suffering is one of the ways that shapes us into becoming more like him. Scarring is not only part of the healing process, it's part of the journey toward becoming a new creature—a stronger, more joyful person.

In Psalm 71, we see the Psalmist lament his trials, and in the same verse, show how God has restored his life.

"Though you have made me see troubles,
many and bitter,
you will restore my life again;

213

from the depths of the earth
you will again bring me up." (Psalm 71:20)

He doesn't hide his past hurts. He isn't ashamed of his scars. He believes God will work through them to bring healing.

Jesus wasn't ashamed of his scars either. After his resurrection, he not only kept his scars, but showed them to his followers as proof. He could have come back without any visible sign of his wounds. After all, Jesus conquered death, so healing his scars would be possible too. Instead, he left the scars as proof of what he endured.

He also showed the scars to his followers. We can't doubt this is the same Jesus who hung on the cross, whose hands and feet were pierced, and who died. His scars were evidence of his death and resurrection, and eyewitnesses recorded it.

Similarly, our scars become a testimony of the trials we've endured. The scars of loss, betrayal, and brokenness may not be visible, but they remain a defining part of who we are and we don't have to hide them. They testify to what we've been through and how God in his mercy brought us through.

TWENTY-FOUR

Starting Over

——————————————————————————

"I think I need to find a job," I said to Sam one day, after looking at our slowly draining bank account.

"You don't have to feel pressure to work," he replied before he left for work. "Take as much time as you need." He pulled me into a hug and then kissed me goodbye.

When I looked at the account, I started to worry, but Sam never did, not when he went through expensive cancer treatments or when we were giving Silas seizure medication that cost $100,000. He believed it would all work out somehow.

The truth was, I didn't know what was next. Life possessed a strange aimlessness and I was stuck in a holding pattern, like an airplane circling an airport, but never actually landing. This was exacerbated by the seemingly innocent questions people asked me when I least expected it.

"Do you work?" a strange man asked me at a party one evening.

When this question came up with people I hardly knew, I didn't know quite how to respond. What you did for a living interested people, unless you were a stay-at-home mom. For some reason, wiping bottoms and making peanut butter sandwiches fail to make for good party conversation.

If my husband was present, he usually interrupted by saying, "She works 24-7 taking care of the family." But this particular time, Sam was absent. I stood alone, shoving a piece of food into my mouth, trying to think of an answer. *Do I use my husband's reply? Or do I say, 'I'm just a mom' in that almost apologetic way that women use?*

Since Silas died, I no longer felt the need to explain what a stay-at-home mom did or to apologize for my role. I replied, "I stay home."

He looked at me, a bored expression flickered across his face, and I saw him search the room for someone else to talk to. He walked away as I stood there, holding a plate of food, wondering what I was doing with my life now. I wasn't going to explain that to a man I hardly knew, who already was looking for a more interesting conversation.

For years, I was a mother who needed to keep her child alive. That was my laser-sharp focus every day. I gave up hobbies and part-time work. I let go of dreams. He needed a full-time caregiver and his mother. I simply had no more space or energy left for anything else.

But now that he was gone, a strange void filled my life. Like a little boat tossed around in the wide ocean, I searched for direction. Everyone had found their way to shore, while the wind and waves pushed me aimlessly around. Losing your purpose created a different kind of grief.

Instead of wallowing in indecision, I decided to find a job and figured at some point, my purpose would show up like a burning bush. Just like on our Colorado horseback ride, it was time to get back in the saddle.

I blindly applied for a random job that sounded tolerable, but for which I had no recent experience. A few weeks later, a rejection form letter arrived in my email inbox. I stared at it and read the words that they had "hired another candidate." Not only had I not gotten picked, I hadn't even been called in for an interview.

Even though I hadn't really wanted the job, the rejection still stung. Never mind that I didn't have the qualifications or the experience for this particular position, I could only focus on the fact that I hadn't even been called. I had tried to move forward and the door slammed in my face.

"Nobody wants to hire me," I complained to Sam.

"That's not true," he said gently. "Most of the people I know get jobs through connections they have, not by applying online to open positions. Maybe you need to think about who you know."

"I don't have connections," I said.

"You *do* have connections," he shot back.

"Who?" I asked, racking my brain for some answer.

"I don't know," he said. "But you know people."

One evening, we had friends over for dinner and the subject of my future came up again. Jonathan and Janelle were incredibly gifted musicians and ambitious risk-takers, the perfect combination for entrepreneurship. I confessed my struggle in finding a job with no recent experience. Instead of offering advice, they encouraged me to create my own opportunity.

"What would you really like to do?" Jonathan asked.

"I'd like to be a writer." I barely could say the words, afraid someone might laugh for admitting something so silly, even though I had been writing for years. But they didn't burst out laughing. Instead, they just listened.

"Why not put your name out there and start offering your writing services?" Jonathan said. "Put your shingle out and see what happens."

When I was a child, my swim teacher tried to teach me to dive. I wasn't afraid of the water, but I didn't like the feeling of falling into the water headfirst and I could not force myself to do it. I knew how to swim and could save myself. The only thing keeping me from diving was me. My teacher did what any good instructor knew to do: she pushed me in. She knew the only way to overcome my fear of falling headfirst was to actually do it. No amount of discussion or rational explanation would make me less afraid.

Our hard experiences are the same. They are the teachers who push us into deep waters when we don't want to jump. They force us to face our fears. These experiences teach us: *You made it through this hard thing and survived. You are strong enough to do this.*

Deciding to write about my grief gave me the chance to process my loss in a safe space, but I hadn't expected it to become the shingle Jonathan recommended. It offered a way for people to see my writing and reach out to me for other kinds of writing work. To my husband's delight, these jobs came from people we knew—the connections he had touted to me months before. I was learning a valuable lesson: the more I focused on taking risks, the more I could see God doing a new thing through those small wobbly steps.

THE TENTH TREASURE

The Gift of Purpose

As I sat at my desk upstairs writing, I could see over the new fence where my stolen purse had been dumped. The power company owned this weed infested strip of land, but left it vacant and teeming with thistles and ground ivy. After our break-in, Sam built a fence, digging holes in the hot sun and nailing up pieces of wood until he'd enclosed our yard and we could no longer see this eyesore. It was a forgotten and purposeless patch, and as a result, the weeds and wild animals quickly claimed it as their own.

That overgrown strip reminded me of our burglary, the loss of Silas, and all the flashbacks wrapped up in those two traumatic days. Despite the painful memories, I wanted to make something useful of the space, to give it an intentional purpose instead of leaving it to the wild. I refused to let this wasteland define my life.

While shopping at the garden center, I saw a row of black raspberry plants. I had always wanted to grow berries on our small property, but the combination of little acreage and the floppy canes made it difficult to find the right space. That's when I thought of it: the patch of land behind the fence. The black raspberry bushes could be planted in that dormant space and use the fence to climb toward the sky. I wasn't sure whether this new space would provide enough sunshine, but it was worth a try.

We planted the tiny bushes, which barely reached our knees, in the hard clay soil. It didn't look like much, but the following year, the bushes grew and produced a small crop of berries. The year after that, the bushes bolted skyward, overpowering the weeds and stretching over the fence. The resulting crop of berries filled buckets.

As I stood under the hot sun, picking berries, letting the juice stain my fingers, I realized we had finally found a purpose for this vacant strip. No longer was it a forgotten wasteland; the bushes produced luscious fruit for our family.

Even more than that, God had shown me a picture of his love. He revealed to me that through the broken pieces of our lives, he could create something new and purposeful. The land that once held bad memories was now reclaimed as fruitful. I knew if God could take an overgrown patch and produce sweet-tasting fruit, how much more could he take the brokenness in my life and make something beautiful from it? From my hurt, God could redeem the shattered parts and restore what looked hopeless. His plan is to give me a hope and future even when everything in my life seems beyond repair.

Jeremiah 29:11 says,

> "'For I know the plans I have for you,' declares the Lord, 'plans to prosper you and not to harm you, plans to give you hope and a future.'"

Although God was giving this promise to Israel, I've seen countless times how the Lord's purpose and plan have unfolded in my life. He hasn't left me in times of brokenness. He did not abandon me when my son died or my husband was sick with cancer. Instead, he restored my life after suffering in the darkest valley. He showed me he was not done writing my story. There was a purpose in my pain.

Sometimes in those parts of our lives where we believe there can be nothing good, God redeems the barrenness and brokenness. He takes our ugly, hopeless places and turns them into something that bears fruit and brings him glory. No matter how much we've suffered, Jesus can take our busted up lives and make them complete again, whole enough for something good to come out of the wasteland. It's a reflection of his power over the hopeless and the heartbroken, the desperate and the despairing. Every time I savor the fruit from those berries, I'm reminded that he can bring redemption to the worst parts of our lives and give it purpose again.

TWENTY-FIVE

Nobody Can Do This for You

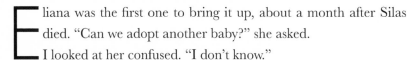

E liana was the first one to bring it up, about a month after Silas
died. "Can we adopt another baby?" she asked.
I looked at her confused. "I don't know."

She went on, "We could even get a baby with Leigh's disease, just
like Silas!"

In her mind, we could pick out a baby like Silas and all our heartache would end. The solution was simple. But the truth was, I hadn't
wanted to talk about adoption again, even though the thought of
bringing home another baby was repeatedly dangled in front of me
like a glittery, bejeweled promise.

Long ago, Sam and I talked about adopting three children, but
when Silas' health issues became overwhelming, we knew we could not
adopt a third child. I didn't have the time or energy to care for another
child. With Silas gone, everything had shifted, but I still hesitated to
embrace a major change. I wasn't sure that the best time to adopt a
baby, or make any life-changing decision, was in the middle of grief.
The thought of going through an emotionally complex process, with
the potential of a failed adoption, overwhelmed me.

"We can't adopt a baby who has Leigh's disease," I said, trying to
let her down gently. "I don't think we're ready for that yet."

She went on pleading, "But I really want another brother with
Leigh's disease! Why can't we just get another brother?"

"Because we can't," I said firmly. It was my parental equivalent of
"because I said so" and I watched as her face fell. In her mind, our
family grief had become a math problem to solve. We were all trying
to work out a solution, but I couldn't explain that life was not like
algebra.

"We can't adopt a baby," I told her softly.

I stood in the kitchen as she turned to leave. *How can I explain to her how complicated grief is? Or how I cannot take away the pain with another baby or walk through an intense emotional adoption process right now?*

In her eight-year-old mind, the answer was clear. The way out of grief was to fill the hole with the same thing we had lost. But I had learned you can't replace one person with another. No matter how many substitutes you try, the hole will still be there. If God was leading us to adopt, he was going to have to make it clear.

To complicate matters, I couldn't seem to figure out what I should do next. I was quickly approaching forty and I no longer had time on my side to decide later. How could I have known, at age twenty-three, that all my plans for the future were going to be burned to dust? That instead, God was going to teach me a lesson about letting go and following him no matter how scared I was of the unknown. This was about trust, but my heart was wounded badly, and I feared anything that could cause more injury.

The answer came in the most unlikely of places: in a celebrity magazine in the middle of an African-American salon. I was watching my daughter get her hair braided, when I started flipping through a glossy entertainment magazine. Even though I didn't care which celebrity was getting married or what dress they wore to the Oscars, I stopped on a gorgeous picture of Gwyneth Paltrow, who was asked about having more kids. She shared the best advice she'd received was from an older lady who told her she shouldn't make the decision based on how hard the newborn stage was, but on who she wanted to have around her Thanksgiving table when she was seventy. The advice-giver noted that sleep deprivation only lasted a few years, but who you have around your table impacted the rest of your life.[4]

When I read that line, I saw our little family of three sitting around the dining room and I longed for something more. Since Silas had passed away, the void of his absence loomed so large, I hadn't envisioned our family beyond today. The question from the magazine opened up a whole new possibility. *Who do I want around my table when I am seventy?*

No one can predict whether they will live to old age, or even to next year. We can't imagine a Thanksgiving thirty years down the road when we haven't even planned for this year's party. But I couldn't put off the decision about whether we would adopt another child. I was quickly approaching midlife and the window of opportunity would slowly be closing. *Am I asking too much to want one more child?* I shut the magazine and put it back in the rack, trying to pretend like someone hadn't just shaken my heart up. *This is a crazy idea.* And then a few seconds later, *Or is it?*

"She's all done," the hairdresser announced as my daughter crawled out of the chair, her hair gelled back into tight braids.

"It looks good," I said, my mind somewhere else. The question from the magazine swirled in my head and I wanted to tell Sam about it. He was always a sounding board for my crazy ideas, but when we walked into the kitchen, Sam was distracted with making dinner and our daughter hovered nearby. I didn't want to discuss it in front of her, at least not yet. What if I changed my mind tomorrow or next week?

We had always been open about our feelings, but grief had made both of us protective of our partner's heart. I was mired in the world of the in-between—feeling conflicted about what I had read and unsure where this was leading.

I didn't tell anybody about the idea for several months. It sat in my brain, buried like a little seed. I feared the idea, terrified of leading us down a path of heartbreak and regret. Love can heal a heart, but love can also wreck it. Adoption was not a straight path, and I knew if we agreed to pursue another adoption, we'd be signing up for an emotional roller coaster ride. In other words, I'd have to risk breaking my heart.

The arduous process required mountains of paperwork, legal hoops to jump through, and a large sum of money. It was also emotionally taxing, especially with the risk of being matched with a baby we might lose. After our family had gone through so much loss, I couldn't imagine heaping more loss on my plate. It was the one obstacle I could not seem to overcome: more loss.

It wasn't until the subject came up on a lunch date that I finally confessed.

"Have you thought about adopting again?" Sam asked.

The words were stuck in my throat, like saying them made them real for the first time. "I've been thinking about it," I said quietly. "I read this magazine article."

Sitting there, looking at my plate, I realized how idiotic I sounded confessing I got life advice from an entertainment magazine. Why couldn't the inspiration have come from somewhere else, like the Bible? With reluctance, I explained the story and ended with, "I think I want more people around our table."

The words weighed heavy, like I was sharing some dark secret. Sam was the one person I confided in completely. I could bounce crazy ideas off of him without fear of being laughed at or criticized. When I asked him, "How about we paint one wall in our dining room a deep teal?" or "What if we knock out the wall in our kitchen and build a window seat?" He always replied, "Yes." While I needed to think about things before committing, he was, for the most part, quick to embrace anything I threw his way. It was one of the reasons I loved him. The fact I had kept this secret from him bothered me. At the same time, I also knew that if I brought it up and then changed my mind, it could hurt him more. Releasing these words felt strange and wonderful and scary at the same time.

"I've been thinking about it ever since I read the article, but I was afraid to tell you. I was afraid you might not feel the same way."

I waited for him to tell me that he didn't want another baby or that he wasn't ready, or maybe, *just maybe*, that he was.

"That's interesting you say that," he replied slowly as we ate. "Because I've been thinking the same thing. I just wasn't sure how you'd feel about it."

"You've been thinking about adoption too?" I said. "I was afraid to say something because I didn't want you to feel like I was trying to talk you into it."

He looked at me and smiled, the same grin that had made my stomach do flip-flops when we were dating.

"I guess if we've been both thinking about it," he said, "that's a good thing."

Just like that, we had made a decision to move forward. I knew most of our friends and family would be ecstatic and at the same time, there might be others who would wonder why, at our age and after all the loss, we wouldn't move on without taking more risks.

But here's the thing: nobody could tell me what was the next right thing after going through something so devastatingly hard. Only I could make this decision to move forward and expand my table.

We knew that the thought of adoption wouldn't have been placed in our minds coincidently. God was nudging us toward a new direction, one that he had already planned for us. We were holding on to faith that he would take us down the path and not let our already battered hearts get too beaten down in the process. In the end, we had to trust that we wouldn't end up with more hurt.

Now that we knew what a broken heart felt like, it took courage to step out in faith and to risk it all for love. But we were willing to try anyway.

THE ELEVENTH TREASURE

The Gift of Faith

On our way home from a school soccer game, I was curious about a new app Sam had downloaded to his phone. It was a test for the enneagram, a popular personality guide that outlined a person's strengths and weaknesses. Within a few minutes, this app was supposed to lead to greater self-discovery. "Can I take the test?" I asked. Sam handed me his phone and said, "Go ahead."

After answering a series of questions, my results indicated I was an enneagram six, the loyalist. This number meant that I was great at championing people, because I was doggedly loyal and loved to support their causes. But then it gave me the bad news: sixes struggled with overwhelming fear and this anxiety colored everything they did. It made them afraid to try new experiences. It produced a worst-case-scenario mentality. It shackled them to what they knew was safe.

"I don't know that I agree with this," I said, a bit miffed that my weaknesses were so blatantly pointed out. It seemed like my test had come out inaccurately. After all, I didn't consider myself an overly fearful person.

"Maybe the test was wrong," Sam said, but something in his voice made me doubt his words.

Later, I picked up a book about the enneagram, determined once and for all to see if the test I had taken was actually right.[5] When I finally reached the chapter about my personality type, I was ready to find proof that I could not be pigeonholed into a specific number. As I pored over the description, my case against being a six crumbled and I saw a clear picture of myself. To make matters worse, I learned that traumatic experiences only confirmed my fears even more. In other words, my greatest weakness had been exacerbated by the realization of my greatest fears. How could I overcome something that is innately part of who I am and proved by my life experiences?

I sat on my bed, book in hand, searching for a solution. Trying to conquer the monster of fear seemed impossible now, except for one thing: I had to learn to trust God completely with my anxieties. The solution to fear was grasping hold of the belief that Jesus would not let me drown when the waves threatened to consume me. In the end, I had to believe that no matter what happened, God still had good planned for me. He was still sovereign over all things. That truth needed to change how I lived.

The same principle is true for all of us. If you're struggling to overcome worry, then the solution is looking toward the one who can take your fears and trusting him with the outcome of each day. The path to moving forward past our fears is always Jesus, the one who can heal our hurts and ease our troubled minds, even when life unravels like a spool of thread. But that kind of faith is not easy. It requires you to forge ahead trusting him, though the way is murky and the future unclear.

Even the writer of Hebrews reminds us that faith involves hopeful confidence in the unseen.

"Now faith is confidence in what we hope for and assurance about what we do not see" (Hebrews 11:1).

Even though we throw the word faith around easily, it doesn't come natural to us. Instead, fear, worry and doubt instinctively dwell in us. Faith, on the other hand, requires us to scale the mountain of fear, trusting in God's plan, even when the heaviness of doubt feels like shackles around our feet. It means recognizing the way fear controls us and then releasing its white-knuckled grip on our lives. It asks that we accept God's plan even when we do not know the outcome. In other words, faith requires us to live differently.

Years ago, I went on a spiritual retreat where we had to write down our fears on paper and throw them into a blazing campfire. Paper after paper was dropped into the fire, but only when I dropped my worry, the one I had been clinging to with clenched fists, did I begin to understand. Letting go meant not only leaving it in God's hands, but also letting it burn to dust so that I couldn't reach in and pick it out of the fire. I had to abandon it there, disintegrating to nothing, and then turn and walk away. I had to choose to trust God.

Since then, I've learned that giving up fear is a daily requirement. It's a deliberate choice that requires me to live in a radical new way. Even when there's no fire to throw my fears into, I can still offer it to Jesus instead of trying to wrestle control for it. Each day, it's an act of the will to give up what I want to hold on to. Only when I let go of my fear will I discover the peace that can be found when I put my faith in a sovereign God.

PART THREE

Beginning Again

She was made for hope
It was woven in the fabric of her soul
Even on the darkest night
She would not give up.

TWENTY-SIX

Choosing Brave

⊙——————————————————————⊙

"We can't get a good fingerprint, let's try again," the lady working the fingerprint machine said.

I stood there, rolling my finger across a digital screen, that promptly rejected the print again. It was clear: I was the problem child of the fingerprinting world. Apparently, I should have been a criminal.

We had been down the adoption path before, so I knew that fingerprinting was particularly tricky for me. I found this out during our first adoption, when I learned I had worn down fingerprints, making it difficult to get a clear picture. Because the state required adoptive parents to submit one good print of each finger for a criminal background check, I had to endure this trial until I passed. The fingerprinting lady tried again, pressing and rolling my finger across the tiny screen that captured the image. Then the machine beeped, rejecting my print again. Until every single finger cleared the test, I could not pass my background check.

This time around, I knew what to expect when I walked into the poorly lit fingerprinting office for our third adoption. A young man with a vacant expression took us back to a room with the fingerprinting machine. My husband stepped forward first and sailed through all ten fingers in less than five minutes.

Then I stepped to the machine for my turn. "I have really poor fingerprints," I told the man. He didn't really acknowledge this news, instead, he asked for my hand and started rolling my fingers across the screen. Several fingers failed and had to be reprinted, but mostly, he was making record time with my terrible prints. We walked out of the office in less than a half-hour.

It seemed like a positive sign that this adoption was going smoothly, almost too smoothly, and I kept wondering when we'd hit our first major detour. During our first adoption, the detour was my husband's cancer. For our second, we waited a long time for a match and eventually ended up switching to a different agency. The delay cost us months and meant we had to redo most of the paperwork.

But unlike our last experience, this adoption was sailing along. Before we even finished our paperwork, the adoption agency asked us to turn in the final documents because they had a birth mom interested in meeting us. She was due in two months. Beyond a handful of family and friends, we hadn't even announced our adoption publicly yet.

When we met Chloe, she was living alone in a small town, single-handedly parenting a toddler. Hardest of all, she had moved away from her family and friends and had zero support other than one neighbor.

Chloe and I began to meet regularly at restaurants for lunch. The more time we spent together, the more she opened up to me about her past. As she began to trust our family, she asked me to be in the delivery room when the baby was born and invited me to her next doctor's appointment. As we chatted over salads and sodas, she confessed she had missed her last checkup because her car had a flat tire. Living in a small town with no public transportation made it almost impossible for a pregnant woman to go anywhere.

When the doctor examined her at the appointment on the day before Christmas Eve, the conversation quickly turned serious. "I think we should induce you today," the doctor said.

"But she's not due for another week," I said. "Why induce her now?"

"She's missed some appointments, so I don't want her going into labor alone and not be able to get to the hospital," the doctor said. She turned to Chloe. "Go home and get your bags packed and come back to the hospital."

When we arrived at Chloe's house, her car sat lopsided in the driveway. The flat tire looked like a melted piece of rubber on the pavement. When I walked in the house, dirty dishes were stacked on every countertop and a skillet sat crusted over with food. She packed a bag to take to the hospital, while her son played on the floor with his toys. My brain had clicked into high gear, the way it always does when I'm checking off all the mental boxes of preparation. I wanted to help Chloe at the hospital since she had no one to be with her. The thought of having the baby alone, without any support, seemed unthinkable. And yet, she needed someone to watch her son. Her only supportive neighbor had declined. I walked back to the car and called Sam while she finished packing.

"I don't know what to do," I said. "She is going to be induced and has no one to take care of her son. Can you help?"

"Of course," he said. "I'll come get him." Even though we were strangers to him, she had no other choice. This was life as a single mother without a support system, a church, or a community. Living alone meant your life was constantly fraught with these kinds of decisions. You were your child's only support and when that failed, there was no safety net. She finished packing while I told her that Sam could take her son until her neighbor was available. Relief flooded her face.

As we arrived at the hospital, I noticed the halls were vacant, a ghost town for the holidays with only the very sickest staying over Christmas. Even the labor and delivery floor contained only one other family. Chloe sat in bed watching TV, looking sick and uncomfortable. Her labor was at a standstill and she couldn't stop vomiting. I did my best to distract her and held the vomit bag when she threw up.

Later, her nurse saw me in the hall and pulled me aside. "I have relatives who adopted a child," she quietly told me. "I hope things work out for you."

I smiled and thanked her and then returned to Chloe's room. Hospital staff needed to treat adoptive parents like any other visitor, and rarely acknowledged my presence. I knew that underneath this neutral front, most workers had feelings on adoption, both for and against it.

When the nurse came into the room on duty, her face revealed nothing.

As the labor dragged on overnight, I tossed and turned on a hard vinyl couch while Chloe tried to sleep without much success. When the doctor arrived the next morning, she noted that the baby had made little progress and started bringing up a possible C-section. Chloe objected. The doctor gave her until noon on Christmas Eve day.

Around lunchtime, the doctor still hadn't come back to check on Chloe, so I told her I was grabbing some lunch. Chloe was still sick to her stomach, so I decided to eat my food in the cafeteria, when I received a text message.

"I'm having a C-section. I want you here," Chloe wrote.

I raced up to her room and arrived as she was being transferred to the operating room. Her eyes were wide with fright, her face frozen with fear. "I'll pray for you," I said, standing next to her while nurses swarmed around us, prepping for surgery. They wheeled Chloe into the operating room where they began setting up for the delivery.

"It's going to be okay," I said to her quietly, but she didn't seem to hear me or anyone. The nurses set up a small curtain that blocked our view of the operation. Chloe lay unusually still, her expression vacant, as the doctor and nurses began chatting like they were meeting for drinks at the bar. The radio was playing in the background as Adele's voice crooned "Hello," a powerhouse love ballad that rankled in this sterile setting. I'm sure Adele never imagined her song would be the anthem for a Caesarian section, but it seemed strangely appropriate after they curtained us off from the action.

Even though I'd been in the delivery room before, I wasn't keen on seeing my first C-section. The doctor and nurses didn't seem to notice Chloe's fear or my own hesitation. They made small talk like they were standing around a water cooler instead of slicing a woman's abdomen open. If I had been Chloe I might have shouted, "Hey! I'm right here! I can hear everything you're saying!" Instead, her face froze tight with fear. I could see the doctor's head on the other side of the curtain as she worked, her glasses splattered with a tiny spotted line of blood. Up until then, the mood had been light, but the conversation had quickly died down as everyone concentrated behind the curtain. Their eyes focused on one spot while the radio played in the background. Blood pooled on the floor near the doctor's feet. I grew lightheaded looking at it, so I glanced away and concentrated on Chloe's vacant face.

Be brave, I told myself. *For her.*

There was a scuffling of noise and a baby's cry erupted from behind the surgical curtain. The nurses rushed over to the side of the operating room where they began to wipe the baby clean. He was a wailing bundle of dark chocolate with a scrunched up face and a body plump with rolls.

"It's a boy," one of the nurses announced. Chloe's face finally registered a flicker of emotion. She smiled weakly while the doctor worked behind the curtain to finish the C-section.

"Would you like to see him?" the nurse asked.

"Yes," I said. I walked over to where he was placed under the warming lamp.

"What will you name him?" the nurse asked me.

I hesitated to say it before the papers were signed, as if saying it kept it from coming true. "His name is Isaac," I replied. It was the name Chloe and I had agreed on weeks before. As an adoptive parent in the hospital, I never knew where I belonged. I was stuck in between two worlds, not quite this child's mother and yet praying to be.

After Chloe and the baby were settled into her hospital room, I went home for Christmas Eve and spent the next morning with Eliana and Sam unwrapping gifts. After lunch, we went to the hospital together, carrying a baby-sized Santa hat for Isaac and Christmas lights to decorate Chloe's room. Her other son was now staying at her neighbor's and Chloe had told me privately that she kept trying to convince her to keep the baby.

Chloe knew from experience that raising a child alone wasn't easy, but she also admitted she was getting texts from friends trying to sway her to parent. Most of these people lived a distance away and would not be the ones up at night or providing a break when she needed some help. Chloe brushed it off. "I'm going to sign those papers," she told us.

On the day Chloe was legally allowed to sign the adoption paperwork, we received a call from our caseworker. "I'm sorry to tell you that Chloe wants more time to decide. She is not ready to sign the papers today."

"Oh, okay. So how soon will she decide?" Sam asked. "How much time does she need?"

I knew we were asking impossible questions, but the timing was difficult. Just yesterday, Chloe had talked about signing the papers. She had seemed certain. We were scheduled to leave for Pennsylvania to see family over the next week. Her indecision made it hard for us to leave.

"I think you should go ahead on your trip," the caseworker said. "If she makes a decision, we'll let you know."

Sam hung up the phone and looked at me. We realized that our adoption was on shaky ground. We thought she seemed so sure, her decision set in stone, even though we knew that nothing about adoption is ever certain. Even so, we had foolishly let our hearts become entangled in this baby's life. We thought the baby was ours and this was our moment of joy after so much grief. But everything had changed with one phone call.

Chloe would be heading home with the baby while we left for Pennsylvania to spend time with family. It was a strange week of waiting for the phone to ring, anticipating some news. But our phones were silent.

When we got home, we called the adoption agency. They hadn't heard from Chloe. When they called her, she told them the news.

She had decided to parent.

THE TWELFTH TREASURE

The Gift of Peace

One winter, we decided to take our daughter on a trip so we could teach her to ski. After a whole day of practicing how to stop and how to turn, our daughter delighted in skiing down easy runs without falling. The slopes had mostly been deserted, which made for ideal skiing conditions.

But around four o'clock in the afternoon, the slopes began to fill with college students from a nearby university. To my amazement, many of them didn't have a clue how to ski and didn't seem to understand how dangerous they were on the slopes. They were crashing into other skiers and veering off into the woods. The gentle slopes became a minefield of accidents.

To avoid a crash, we tried a different slope that we hoped would be less busy. The wide hill seemed promising with ample room for us to ski around others who had fallen. What we couldn't see yet was the end of the run, where the slope suddenly narrowed, did a hard right turn, and dropped steeply. As we came to the ninety-degree turn, we noticed beginning skiers could neither make the sharp turn nor stop, so we slowed down and watched as one skier after another bit the dust.

"We need to come up with a plan to get to the end of this run," Sam said.

Eliana had done well learning to ski, but the steep hill combined with the heavy amount of crashes, would make it a tricky section to descend without an accident.

"Eliana you're going to go first, because if I go first, I won't be able to see you if you fall," he explained. "Instead, I'll ski behind you and tell you what to do. You won't be able to see me, but you can listen to my voice."

With this plan, we started down the steep slope. At first, everything went smoothly. Eliana listened to her father's voice instructing her down the steep descent. But out of nowhere, a reckless skier almost sideswiped her, then crashed in her path. Distracted and afraid, she bolted down the hill like a rocket trying to flee from danger. By the time Sam realized it, he was too late. She lost control and crashed just before finishing the run.

Although she wasn't hurt from the accident, she learned a valuable lesson. Instead of taking the slow and steady path guided by her father, she listened to the voice of fear and lost control.

Likewise, when we feel like our lives are out of control, we are prone to wander off and go our own way. Instead of following the voice of our heavenly Father, we listen to the voice of fear, because life has wounded us deeply. It's our natural instinct to flee from danger, but instead of running to our Father, we run from him. We reject his promises. We ignore the peace and safety he offers us.

When I bought into the lie that nothing good could happen to me, I accepted a false truth that God's goodness would not prevail in a season of darkness. I believed that somehow other people deserved good things, but I did not. It's tempting to buy into the lie that there's something wrong with us or we're not good enough to be blessed. With that perspective, we're effectively shackled from making any progress for the kingdom of God. It's vital to keep listening to the Father's voice when our fears and doubts threaten to topple us. Every anxiety can feel like a deepening of an already tender wound, but as God guides us, he can also give us an incredible peace that there is a plan beyond what we can understand. He still has good things for us and he will not lead us astray. He speaks life-giving truth through his Word and through time alone with him.

In Proverbs 3:5-6, the writer gives instruction on how to trust God when we don't have peace about the future.

"Trust in the Lord with all your heart
and lean not on your own understanding;
in all your ways submit to him,
and he will make your paths straight."

By giving our futures to God, we will experience the gift of peace, even while our paths may feel anything but secure. He will show us that he hasn't left us alone. He is guiding us toward straight paths, if we will only listen.

○————————————————————○

TWENTY-SEVEN

The Center of Loss and Joy

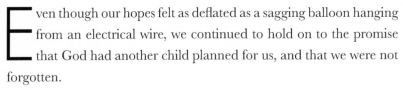

Even though our hopes felt as deflated as a sagging balloon hanging from an electrical wire, we continued to hold on to the promise that God had another child planned for us, and that we were not forgotten.

Several months went by before we got another call about a birth mom who was a single mother with several small boys at home. Tara was due in a few months and was eager to have an adoption plan in place. We drove several hours to a women's care center and sat in a windowless room as Tara shared her life story and told us how determined she was to go through with this adoption.

A few weeks later, Tara was scheduled for a C-section, so we packed our bags for the hospital. When we arrived, the hospital was filled with babies in rolling bassinets and people carrying balloons announcing, "It's a boy!" The hospital gave us a separate room from the birth mother where we waited during the C-section. Finally, a nurse appeared and said, "The baby is here. Do you want to go see him?"

We followed her to the nursery, where another nurse huddled around his tiny, brown body. Wailing at the top of his lungs, he shook with the uncoordinated jerkiness of a newborn.

Later we visited with Tara, who was in good spirits despite having endured a C-section. She admitted that the birth dad and his mother were pressuring her to parent now that the baby had arrived. Although he was the one who brought her to the hospital for the C-section, he refused to go into surgery with her. I saw the heartbreak in her eyes as she said, "He just dropped me off at the door." She lay back on her pillow looking at us. "I'm still going through with the adoption," she said.

Tara usually visited with the baby during the day for a few hours, while we took the night shift so she could rest. One evening, Tara requested the baby and several hours later, still hadn't brought the baby back to our room. We were tired so we told the nurse, "We're going to bed, just wheel the baby down to us when she wants to sleep."

About three a.m., the baby turned up in our room again. We gave him a bottle, and swaddled and soothed him until he fell back to sleep. The next morning Tara could sign the adoption papers and we would be allowed to leave with our new son.

The next day we woke up and I headed to the shower while Sam sat in the recliner rocking the baby. I was already thinking through details that I had not taken care of yet. Something had told me to hold off.

If the baby comes home, I told myself, *then we'll move the desk and set up the nursery. If, if, if.*

Just a week before, I stocked up on new baby onesies, the kind that looked like they'd fit a doll. Though I felt positive about Tara's resolve, I left the tags on in case they needed to be returned. I didn't want to make assumptions about how this adoption would turn out.

If it happens, then I'll take them off.

If, then was where I had been living for so long, I didn't know what I'd do when the papers were finally signed. I was ready to close this chapter of waiting, eager to get home and become a family.

When I finished blow-drying my hair in the bathroom, I heard Sam talking on the phone, concern in his voice. Though I couldn't hear the conversation through the bathroom door, his tone alarmed me. I opened the door as he set his cell phone down. He stood there, the baby nestled in his arms, staring at me with a mixture of shock and sadness.

"What is wrong?" I asked.

The color dropped out of his face as he spoke quietly, "She changed her mind. She is keeping the baby."

He was holding the baby as the words hung in the air. Bad news has a way of slowing time down, making everything murky, the same way you feel when you're swimming underwater.

But you're holding the baby, I said to myself. *You're holding the baby.*

"I don't understand," I said. "I thought she was sure. What did the caseworker tell you?"

"She told me that Tara sent an email this morning saying she wanted to parent and that she was sorry. Then the caseworker wondered if I had any questions, so I asked her if I was supposed to call the nurse to take the baby back to her," Sam said. "And she asked if the baby was still with me in the room so I told her, 'Yes, I'm holding him.'"

Sam's face was like the sky during a July thunderstorm, when the clouds turned a dark shade of charcoal. Our world had shifted in one call.

"She never dreamed I'd still be holding him," he added.

Sam cradled the baby in his arms as I sat on the hospital bed stunned. I could no longer say, "If we bring him home." The answer was no.

Sam walked to the bassinet with the baby swaddled tightly in a hospital blanket. He slept peacefully, unaware of the drama swirling around him, an innocent bystander at the center of loss and joy.

"Did you want to say goodbye before I call the nurse to take him back?" he asked.

No, I thought, my fists clenched. But when I turned to look at him, I saw his tiny lips and the gentle curl of his eyelashes and I said quietly, "Yes." I touched the soft wisps of his hair as I whispered, "Goodbye."

My husband laid the baby in his bassinet and put his hand on his head. He began praying for the child, a blessing on his life, a final goodbye. Then he called the nurse to take the baby back to Tara.

"I can't watch the nurse wheel him out of the room," I said, "I just can't."

There was no place for me to go except the bathroom, so I waited there. Behind closed doors, I heard Sam explain that we would be leaving the hospital since Tara had decided to parent. The nurse rolled the bassinet out of the room and down the hall and like that, the baby was gone. I slowly opened the door and sat down on the bed.

"What do you want to do?" Sam asked.

Suddenly, I no longer belonged in the hospital and I felt like a foolish little girl who had been caught playing dress up in her mother's clothes. I hadn't had a baby, nor was I leaving with one.

"Let's go," I said as I started to pack.

As much as I wanted to know why Tara had changed her mind, I didn't have the heart to ask her. Long ago, a wise soul told me that when it comes to adoption, someone always goes home with a broken heart. This time, it would be us.

When we left our room, I looked down the hall toward Tara's room. Part of me wanted to say goodbye, but I didn't know how to do it, so I turned away and walked toward the elevator.

I stopped to look at the gift basket of goodies I had planned to give to Tara. It was stocked with treats, but it seemed a waste to throw them out. As we walked outside into the warm spring morning, the valet parking attendants, who barely looked out of high school, noticed our basket.

"That looks good," one of them joked.

My husband stopped and wheeled around. He held out the basket and asked, "Do you want some?"

"No, no," the young man replied, his face flushing with color.

"No, really. Can you eat on the job?" Sam asked.

"Yeah," the young man said.

"Then pick whatever you want." Sam held out the basket again. The attendants paused to see if he was serious, and then reached into the basket and pulled out candy and chips. It was their lucky day, even if it hadn't been ours.

As we piled our things in the car for the long trip home, we saw the empty car seat in the back, one more reminder of our loss. I thought through what we could have said to change Tara's mind. I recounted our conversations, what we should or shouldn't have done. If I had said something else, would it have changed things? *If, then* can be a very terrible place to live when life goes badly, but I couldn't keep myself from going there.

The problem with this mentality is that it doesn't change the past. There was nothing we could have done to alter the outcome. But the human side of me wanted a logical explanation. I wanted to know *why*.

Then I remembered the prayer I had been saying for weeks: *If* this was not the right baby for us, *then* I asked that God would stop it from happening. The answer was clear, but not what I wanted. Why was accepting no so hard? Sometimes hanging on to hope wasn't an act of will, it was an act of faith.

Remembering my prayer, I realized the *if, then* mentality only made sense when we saw the hand of God working through our lives. If God had wanted it to happen, then we would be holding a baby. But we weren't. As hard as that might be, I needed to accept that his plan would be better than the one I was grieving. Maktoob—*it was written*—meant that we were not the ones chosen as parents for this child. Only in light of God's complete sovereignty over our lives could I understand that his will was the best thing that could ever happen to us. To someone who doesn't believe in a sovereign God, this might seem crazy. But to us, it was enough of an answer. A sovereign God gives order to life's chaos when human answers don't make sense.

Though we didn't understand why it had happened, we trusted that God was good, even in disappointing circumstances. We held on to the belief that God's intentions for our lives were still good, whether we received good news or bad.

When I held on to these promises, I didn't ask *if* God was good and *if* he loved me. I knew he was and he did. And I knew the *if, then* questions would all be fulfilled in him. Through the joy, and the sorrow, and everything in between.

THE THIRTEENTH TREASURE

The Gift of Perseverance

I have never been a runner. But in this season of waiting on a baby, I was running, though I was terrible at it. Every time I got on the treadmill, I started strong, but after hitting a certain time I found myself thinking, *I can't go on. I'm too tired.* My body hurt, the sweat ran down my arms, and I wanted to quit.

Sometimes I slowed down the treadmill so I could walk, but other times, I started playing a little mental game with myself. I told myself if I could just go another minute, then I could stop. Then a minute would pass and I would repeat the same thing.

I knew if I yelled, "Go 10 more minutes!" I would have given up. Ten minutes was impossible when my body cried out to stop, but one minute seemed possible. At the time, I hadn't realized that what I was learning was a lesson in perseverance. The process of running showed me how to keep going, to push through the pain, even when I thought I couldn't go on.

Despite my body's protests, I was learning how to persevere. When everything in me desperately wanted to quit, I kept going, even when I pleaded for relief. That didn't mean I was always successful, but little by little, I ran longer. During some runs, I quit altogether and then felt disappointed in myself for not sticking it out longer. But other times, I had small victories. I was able to go another minute. And another. And another.

According to the Oxford English Dictionary, perseverance is described as "doing something despite difficulty or delay in achieving success."[6] For the apostle Paul, perseverance directly resulted from enduring suffering.

"Not only so, but we also glory in our sufferings, because we know that suffering produces perseverance; perseverance, character; and character, hope" (Romans 5:3-4).

In other words, when we experienced pain, we learned how to persevere, and perseverance eventually led to hope. Because perseverance was the result of suffering, it always seemed like a difficult lesson learned only through the fire of trials. It was a good trait to acquire, but I didn't want to go through hardship to obtain it.

As I learned to persevere in running, I was starting to see the trait in a different way. The longer I endured the pain, the stronger I became and the more hope I gained that I could make it to the end. Perseverance, then, was a gift that produced other gifts in the process. According to Paul, perseverance produced character, and character produced hope. Though it might be nice to have a life of ease where there was no suffering, an easy life meant we wouldn't learn to persevere under pressure.

It takes great courage to go another minute, or another hour, or another day, when you feel like giving up. But perseverance only asks you to commit to keep going now. If we continue faithfully, then little by little, we will not only learn what perseverance is, but we will grow in character and hope too.

TWENTY-EIGHT

Made for Hope

T hat summer passed like a hot Sunday in August. We didn't hear
from the adoption agency and I tried to forget about the babies
we didn't adopt. It was hard not to count the months, to remember how old they were. I couldn't help dwelling on their mothers,
struggling alone, cuddling tiny infants who cried at night. Even though
I knew that God's plan was the best one, it didn't stop the hurt of rejection and the slow dying of broken dreams. I hung on to the promise
that there would be another baby out there and that he'd come at
the right time. Another lesson in perseverance and hope. During that
summer of waiting, I remember wondering if I had been foolish to try
to add more people to my future Thanksgiving table.

Maybe this isn't meant to be after all.

Sam and I went to our favorite café for lunch on a brilliant summer
day, a place within walking distance of our house. We sat next to a
huge window that looked out onto the street and ordered soup and
salads. When my phone rang, the name of our adoption agency came
up on the screen and my heart jumped.

Because it was too loud to hear the conversation in the café, I slipped
outside into the sunshine. Sam waited at the table inside, watching me
through the window as our caseworker told us the news: They had a
new birth mom interested in us. Would we be willing to meet with her?

"Yes!" I said as Sam watched me from inside the restaurant.

I walked back into the restaurant, sat down, and told Sam the news.
We mulled over the details as we ate soup and bread. Things had taken
an abrupt turn since we walked in the restaurant carrying a heaviness
that we could not shake. This café was our little calm away from the
storm, a place where we could get away from the world for an hour, by

pretending that the real world, and our failed adoptions, didn't exist. But with one phone call, some promise for us dawned and the shape of our conversation changed to something hopeful. We didn't know what the future held, but for now, there was the shimmering light of hope.

We met the birth mom in a country diner, the type of place where they served breakfast all day, and piled eggs and potatoes high on shiny plates. We were crammed in the front table next to the big window that overlooked a busy street. She was different from the moment we met, full of smiles and laughter. She didn't break down into tears as she shared her story. Instead, she seemed upbeat, hopeful, like this was the making of something new.

During one of our lunches together, Nicole asked us, "Would you like to be in the delivery room?"

Witnessing the beginning of a baby's life was an incredible privilege, but I couldn't help but think of Chloe and baby Isaac, the blood smeared across the doctor's glasses and the moment when we got the phone call saying she decided to parent. Then there was Tara and the revelation at the hospital, when Sam was holding the baby and found out the news. The answer was no.

All these failed adoptions led me to believe that it was much easier to build walls around our hearts rather than open them to potential heartbreak. Only a rare person can say yes without weighing the consequences. Love may be worth the risk, but when you've been hurt, you never forget it. Even so, we looked at each other and I said, "Yes."

The months raced by as Nicole neared her due date. During the final weeks, I came down with a nasty cold and cough, evidence of my body weakening under stress. Although there was nothing I could do to change the impending decision, I knew this wasn't about me. It was about saying yes to love.

Even while we trusted God with the outcome, I was torn about whether I should prepare the baby's room, afraid of facing more heartbreak and having to pack away the baby clothes yet again. On the outside, I remained optimistic when people asked how things were going. But on the inside, I was quaking with fear.

I admitted to Sam, "If this one doesn't go through, I'm not sure I'll have the strength to go on with this process."

It was the first time I confessed that I was ready to give up on our dream of adopting another child. How many more times could I be pummeled by life's blows and keep getting up? I knew, no matter how much I hoped, wished, or wanted a baby, it was out of my hands. This was my last attempt at expanding our table. Sam listened quietly. He wasn't ready to give up until he knew the outcome of this situation. But the question hung over him too.

On the day of Nicole's induction, I walked into the hospital with a strange trepidation. *Will I walk out empty-handed, like before? Or will I leave with a new baby?* I pushed the questions down and walked on. No one could give me the answers I needed. No one could do this for me. Even if this adoption didn't work out, I knew that life would move on. I could focus on my work and writing. I had a daughter at home who needed me. But there was a deep-seated longing for another child and nothing could erase that desire.

When we walked into the birthing room, Nicole was all smiles, even on delivery day. Whatever I was facing, she was facing something bigger, and it only made sense that the two of us—both mothers—both longing for life to be different, would somehow band together.

The labor dragged on all day with little progress. Since the hospital was located in our town, we stepped out around dinnertime to surprise Eliana at her first basketball game.

While at the game, Nicole texted us that she had dilated more and that we should "get back ASAP. It's time."

As we piled into the car and sped down the road, I texted back, "We are hurrying. You're doing great!"

"Come on baby mama and baby daddy," she replied.

We made it in time for her to push and all of us crowded around the bed, cheering her on.

"You can do this!" we screamed. "You're doing great!" Like a bunch of rowdy fans at a sports competition, we cheered her on until the last big push when the baby appeared, wailing from the shock of a new world. It was a boy. The doctor handed him to Nicole and she held him as we marveled at how perfect he looked with a thick mane of dark hair and milky brown skin.

We took turns holding him, still caught up in the excitement of the delivery, but the upcoming decision hung over our heads like an impending storm. I pushed the thought away, because for now, there was only this tiny baby.

We named him Zion, a Hebrew name that meant *where God dwells*. The birth mother wanted us to care for Zion while we stayed at the hospital in a separate room, but she also wanted to spend some time with him.

"Of course," we said. "Just let us know when you want us to bring him over."

Her request didn't surprise me. This was the hardest decision she'd ever have to make. I also knew, no matter how hard I tried, I had no control over the outcome. It was out of my hands.

I had tried to analyze our other failed adoptions from every angle, tried to see what we did wrong, and every time I came up empty. There are times in life when human logic is not enough, when we don't find answers to our questions, when we have to accept that what we did, or didn't do, was meant to be in the end. This idea that God had written our days was something I was learning to embrace. Strangely enough, I had come to a place of peace with those answers, even though it was a hard reality to grasp.

As I looked at this little boy's face cradled in my arms, I knew I had to be brave. Sometimes hope looks like holding a baby you don't know will be yours. Other times it looks like accepting the hard road of rejection, without any answers as to why.

The next day, the time came for our birth mother to make a decision. Our caseworker showed up, paperwork in hand, and explained that she was going to our birth mother's room, to see if she had made a decision.

We sat in our hospital room, in silence, waiting. The minutes on the clock in our room slowly ticked by. I knew she would be agonizing over signing the papers. The act of choosing adoption was always tinged with sadness because someone ended up gaining what the other person lost. As I waited, my phone rang with text messages from friends asking if she signed. Our community of support was anxiously waiting for some news, impatient to know how this story ended too. But after everything, I had learned that this story wasn't my story. It was God's story, and somehow, in giving up control, I sacrificed everything—my future, my heart, this outcome. This kind of trust was actually surrender, when everything in me cried for control. But this was one place I had none.

After what seemed like an eternity, the caseworker finally came back into the room. "She signed," she said.

Sam turned to me and wrapped his arms around my waist. She pulled out the paperwork for us to sign as we sat down at the small hospital table. After going through a pile of paperwork, she smiled and said, "Congratulations." Then she left our room. Zion was ours.

As soon as she closed the door, I began to sob. Not a little trickle of tears, but the big heaving sobs of someone who has experienced a great wave of something that has broken inside them. I had not known the tears hid there, but as soon as she left, something crumbled inside me, like a dam that could not hold in the water anymore.

I sobbed into Sam's shirt as he cried too. If someone had walked in on that moment, they might have thought we had received the worst news of our lives. But I have discovered that the best news and the worst news often look the same. Our hearts feel joy and pain differently, but our bodies' reactions are the same. We were made for hope, it was woven into the fabric of our souls, and in the end, hope was what kept us clinging to the belief that we would find our child. Tears are not only for sadness, but for overwhelming joy. In this moment, I could not cry enough of them.

THE FOURTEENTH TREASURE

The Gift of Redemption

I had forgotten about the daffodils in my basement. After a long winter, the centerpiece looked completely dead in the shadows of this dark place, but something held me back from tossing it completely. When I left the plant in the basement, I was hoping for some small sign of life, something to sustain me through difficult days and bitter tears of waiting.

I looked down at the barren soil and saw it: under the dead leaves, tiny points of green were pushing through the dirt. Daffodils. Though I could not understand it, these bulbs had the right conditions to grow, even when everything seemed hopeless.

In our basement, I realized that beauty could emerge out of the dark places and dead spaces. God could use the barren soil of our lives to grow something extraordinary. The beauty of redemption is that our God is a God of dead things, broken lives, and hopeless situations. He shows us that in the midst of pain, there can be treasures in the darkness, gifts of hope we discover, like flowers growing in the shadows. There could be joy in the night, hope piercing through our scars. As I picked up the basket and held it up in the light, I realized those dead spaces in our lives might be something redeemed, made new, growing again. Maybe this is the biggest gift of all: that after the hurt, we can still find hope.

This seems impossible for us, but God is in the business of impossible things. He raised the dead and healed people with incurable conditions. Jesus saved sinners from the curse of hell through his sacrifice on the cross. He conquered death and came back from the grave, so that we could have eternal life. If he can do those impossible things, then he can take our broken hearts, even when they seem beyond repair, and not only heal them, but remake them in a way we can't even understand. How is it possible that we become even more whole after loss?

It doesn't erase the bad things that happen to us. This world is still broken. We still suffer from the Fall. The one thing we can trust is that God is sovereign even in the brokenness of this world and one day, he will make everything right again. He gives us the hope of heaven when he lives inside us.

Colossians 1:27 says,

> "To them God has chosen to make known among the Gentiles the glorious riches of this mystery, which is Christ in you, the hope of glory."

In this verse, Paul tells us that the mystery of God's plan—for Christ to live in us—gives us the hope of glory. We do not have to give in to despair that our disappointments will last forever. Instead, this hope gives us confidence that someday we'll live in heaven with Jesus and all things will be made right. Because Christ is in us, we are made to have hope—the promise of eternity dwells within us. His hope heals us, not because we're in control, but because we trust in a God who not only holds our future, but redeems all of it.

That's where we find the good news—in the stories of redemption. Our story, with all its pain and brokenness, does have a happy ending. It's the promise of a story that does not end in broken pieces, but in wholeness and hope, and finally this: no more goodbyes.

EPILOGUE

THE FIFTEENTH TREASURE

The Gift of Rebirth

We painted the walls in Silas' old bedroom a sky blue and hung silky curtains to match. The room had been transformed, and for the last few years, I'd been writing next to the bedroom windows where Silas used to look outside. I watched squirrels play on the old maple and birds rest on the power line that runs up to the window's edge. I witnessed snow falling on our black raspberry bushes and budding branches dancing in the wind. I poured my heart out into words in this room and sat in the sacred space of quiet. But after four years, the time had come to transform the room again.

A new face joined us around the dinner table for Thanksgiving that year. Our Zion, the missing puzzle piece that fit perfectly into our family, became officially ours. His chubby smile had brought life to our family again, but I also recognized that brokenness was part of the story too. That's always the way life worked—brokenness and healing were two sides of the same coin.

As the light danced across my desk, I packed pencils and papers, pictures frames, and scraps of paper. I thought of all the words I've poured out here as a way to keep the memories of Silas alive. Now the room was becoming something new again, just as my heart had too. This is the beauty of a redeemed life—we find hope in dark places, light coming through the cracks of deep brokenness. Rebirth is about second chances, our lives being made new again, the opportunity to begin again.

But I also recognized that new beginnings were only possible through Jesus' resurrection. He highjacked death through his resurrection and gave us new life. His victory gives us hope in the midst of our own brokenness and the darkness of death. Our story is not over. There is always hope beyond what we can see.

As we start to see our lives through the lens of redemption, then it transforms how we interpret all of life, the good and bad, the joy and the sorrow. Rather than focusing on our circumstances, we begin to change our focus to his story.

We no longer lament the difficulties in the same way, but we see how it has deepened our love for Jesus. We embrace a bigger purpose behind the pain—one that focuses on an eternal perspective. We keep our eyes fixed on the unseen, the eternal weight of glory, which will erase all the pain and sadness from our lives forever.

At some point, hope allows us to move forward so we can begin to let go of everything that holds us back, including our dreams for what might have been. We might fight and rail against letting go, we might lament and mourn, but ultimately, our rebirth is part of our story, showing how God transforms us through brokenness. It means trusting that he will redeem all our experiences by taking our lives out of the ashes and making something beautiful out of it.

He has written our story and it is a story of redemption and hope. Like David, we hold on to God's promises that remind us our story is no accident and all our days are planned. It was maktoob that I wrestled with in my grief. But it was also this idea that gave me peace. Psalm 139:16 says,

> "Your eyes saw my unformed body
> all the days ordained for me
> were written in your book
> before one of them came to be."

As I looked at Zion, sleeping in my arms, I saw how God had taken all the pain and loss and written a new story. God's unconditional love had never failed me, not once, on this journey. It's more than I deserved.

As the dying light from outside softened across his forehead, I rested my hand on him and gave him one last kiss before laying him down in his crib. Hope had healed us. Hope had remade us. In the quiet of this moment, I hung on to all that we'd become and all that we are yet to be.

ACKNOWLEDGEMENTS

I'm indebted to so many people who made this book possible. First, I'm extremely grateful for the support and love from my family. Sam, thank you for sacrificing so I could have time to write and for believing in me when I doubted myself. Without your help, this book wouldn't exist. You are the best husband a girl could ask for.

Thanks to Eliana and Zion for giving me time to work in my writing dungeon and for inspiring me to be a better mom. You make me so proud and being called your mom is one of the greatest gifts.

I'm also indebted to my friends and fellow writers, Christy Cabe and Lori Clounie. You both saw promise in these stories early on and encouraged me to keep writing. I'm so lucky I get to call you friends.

To my hope*writer friends, especially Vanessa Luu, Bekah Bowman, and Rachel Pieh Jones. Even though we are spread out across the globe, your words and friendship have been the inspiration I needed to finish strong.

I'm grateful to all the people who helped make this book come to life. Kristen Ingebretson, your design for this book is beautiful. Thank you for bringing your talent and creativity to this project. To Jaci Miller, my editor, thank you for sharpening this story and pushing me to be a better writer. To Jeff Jacobson and Vanessa Luu, thank you for your writing help, but even more for your encouragement as I neared the finish line.

To my church community, friends, family and neighbors: I'm grateful for those who have shown us Jesus' love through so many difficulties. You've shown up and poured out. You've made meals, helped with our needs, and prayed for us. Community is essential in grief. I cannot name you all, but I am thankful for the priceless ways you've impacted me.

Most importantly, I am thankful for the grace and hope that Christ gives me daily and for his unconditional love that has held me up through the storms of life. This book exists to give glory to him.

MY GIFTS TO YOU
(made with love)

Markdown: ○———————————————————————○

Made for Hope Manifesto Printable

20 Ways to Pray for Yourself Printable

15 Bible Verses to Inspire Hope Printable

Seven-Day Grief Journal

24 Ways to Remember a Loved One Who Has Passed Away

These resources are available at **SaraRWard.com**

RESOURCES ON GRIEF AND LOSS

Walking with God through Pain and Suffering by Timothy Keller

Holding on to Hope: A Pathway through Suffering to the Heart of God
by Nancy Guthrie

A Grace Disguised: How the Soul Grows through Loss by Jerry Sittser

A Grief Observed by C.S. Lewis

Good Grief by Granger Westberg

Option B: Facing Adversity, Building Resilience, and Finding Joy
by Sheryl Sandberg and Adam Grant

NOTES

Chapter 2

1. Joshua Prager, "Is Our Suffering God's Will?" (May 22, 2013), *Cable News Network*: cnn.com/2013/05/22/opinion/prager-our-suffering-gods-will.

Chapter 16

2. Barbara King, "When Animals Mourn: Seeing Our Grief is Not Uniquely Human," (April 11, 2013), *National Public Radio*: npr.org/sections/13.7/2013/04/11/176620943/when-animals-mourn-seeing-that-grief-is-not-uniquely-human.

Chapter 20

3. Brené C. Brown, *Daring Greatly: How the Courage to Be Vulnerable Transforms the Way We Live, Love, Parent, and Lead* (New York: Gotham, 2012).

Chapter 25

4. To my knowledge the interview appeared in *People* magazine, but I could not find the original source.

5. Ian Morgan Cron and Suzanne Stable, *The Road Back to You* (Downers Grove: IVP Books, 2016).

Chapter 27

6. Oxford Dictionary online: lexico.com/en/definition/perseverance.

ABOUT THE AUTHOR

Sara R. Ward is a wife and mom to three children, including a son who passed away from Leigh's disease in 2012. She writes about grief, child loss, adoption, and faith on sararward.com. She is a writer for Adoption.com and has been published in the *Today Show Parenting Team, Focus on the Family* and *Homeschooling Today*. Sara also writes poetry and is an award-winning playwright.

Receive free resources by joining Sara's email list at sararward.com

Facebook: @sararwardauthor

Instagram, Twitter and Pinterest: @sararward

Made in the USA
Monee, IL
24 February 2022